OUR
UNDERWATER
WORLD

OUR UNDERWATER WORLD

igloo

First published in 2010
by Igloo Books Ltd
Cottage Farm
Sywell
NN6 0BJ
www.igloo-books.com

ISBN 978-085734-254-6

B044 0810

Authors:
Karen Farrington
Sandra Forty
Dr Patrick Hook

Printed and manufactured in China

CONTENTS

INTRODUCTION

Turbulent or calm, tropical or icy cold, there is something comfortingly familiar about the planet's seas that bring fish for food, waves for sport and a far-off horizon to lure the willing traveller.

But in reality the oceans are a world apart from our own; deeper, darker and stranger than we can conceive.

The part of the ocean that we usually envisage, illuminated by the sun and alive with creatures and plants, is only the skimpy top layer. Beneath lies a vast coal-black arena that's home, to animals that are quite simply the stuff of nightmares. There are giant squid with eyes the size of dinner plates, viper fish with fangs so large they are not able to close their mouths and a whole host of creatures big and small whose bodies generate an eerie glow through clever chemical responses.

For them home is a hostile environment that we hardly see and can never fully experience. Scientists and documentary makers struggle to penetrate the cold, the dark and the lack of oxygen. New marine species crop up with regularity, as if to underline the fact that comparatively little is known about what really goes on in the leagues that lie below a dappled ocean surface.

Yet perhaps aspects of the oceans that are well known to scientists give us even more cause for concern.

On the ocean floor there are regular shifts in the tectonic plates, those interlocking puzzle pieces that comprise the Earth's surface. Some of these are large enough to begin mighty earthquakes that in turn launch deadly tsunami surges that will engulf the unwary on far distant shorelines.

Ocean life is dominated by currents and winds that in turn bring the world's weather pattern. Every so often there's a glitch that will bring excessive rain, drought or even decimate fish supplies, leaving animals and communities that depend on them bereft.

Then there is climate change, a phenomenon that is causing long-standing polar ice to melt and consequently bringing about a hike in sea levels. No one can say for sure why it is happening and where it will end but there's certainty that low-lying communities across the world will be particularly badly affected.

A rampant fishing industry that has left stocks of once abundant fish at dangerously low concentrations, a generous seepage of industrial chemicals from land and ships and a propensity to use the open sea like a giant dustbin means the oceans are not the pristine waters they once were. They are an immediate threat to the ecosystems that exist in the oceans.

▼ *A shoal of cow breams is tossed about in the shallows by the turbulent waves of the Mediterranean Sea.*

The Oceans

More than two thirds of the earth is covered in water. The salt waters of the world's vast oceans account for most of it and, while we have learned much about what happens in the dry 29 per cent of the earth's surface that we inhabit, and even in the universe beyond it, there is still plenty to discover about those vast tracts beneath the waves.

▲ *A spectacular view of the Earth as seen from space.*

THE OCEANS

It is not only difficult to see what's going on down in the ocean's depths, it is a challenge to even imagine it. Hidden under enormous volumes of water are numerous peaks and volcanoes, including the most extensive mountain range on earth which is concealed in the depths of the Atlantic Ocean.

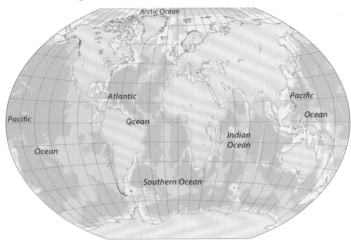

▲ *This illustration shows the positioning of the Earth's oceans.*

Called the Mid-Atlantic Ridge, it runs north to south down the ocean's center for 10,000 km (6,213 miles). And if you thought Everest was the world's tallest mountain, think again. The Pacific island of Mauna Kea hides two thirds of its bulky skirt beneath the shore line so boasts a total tip to toe height of 9,449 m (31,000 ft), some 600 m (almost 2,000 ft) higher than the Nepalese title holder.

Beyond just being breathtaking geographic phenomena, oceans are key to our very survival. Each one is a giant and hugely complex ecosystem, co-dependent on its constituent parts. Every aspect of ocean life – including the tides, winds, warmth, currents and, of course, the marine life held within – operates inside an individual set of rules. Nothing functions in isolation. One catastrophe is likely to beget another in domino fashion in the unfathomable deep.

Many of the causes and effects of even minor oceanic changes are still barely understood by scientists and some are, quite probably, entirely misunderstood and wrongly interpreted. New discoveries are being made all the time, with each revelation having a bearing on our understanding of everything else.

Life on Earth first evolved in the oceans. Today, it is ocean life that is feeling the acute pressure of the pending environmental crisis. A degree or two of extra warmth, a leap in the levels of toxicity or an unsustainable plundering of its riches, has left water-borne environments at risk and any one of these factors could spark a dangerous chain reaction

Yet despite troubling reports to the contrary, the world's seas are still teeming with life. We can speculate that it is not as abundant as it once was but it is there, evident from the shallows to the murky depths. That fact seems more curious still given that ocean water is salty. Who would expect nature to dictate that some of the world's most fascinating and downright strange creatures would be happiest in the stinging waters of the open seas?

▶ *This area of the Indian Ocean near Meemu Atoll in the Maldives is teeming with life.*

▼ *On April 20, 2010, an explosion at an oil well in the Gulf of Mexico resulted in a major oil spill.*

▼ *Heavy seas and climate change contribute to melting icebergs in Antarctica with many experts predicting rising sea levels as a consequence.*

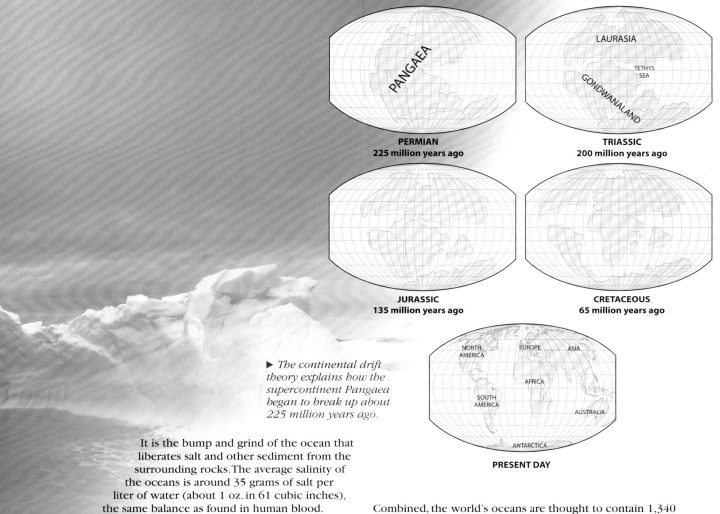

PERMIAN
225 million years ago

TRIASSIC
200 million years ago

LAURASIA
TETHYS SEA
GONDWANALAND

PANGAEA

JURASSIC
135 million years ago

CRETACEOUS
65 million years ago

NORTH AMERICA
EUROPE
ASIA
AFRICA
SOUTH AMERICA
AUSTRALIA
ANTARCTICA

PRESENT DAY

▶ *The continental drift theory explains how the supercontinent Pangaea began to break up about 225 million years ago.*

It is the bump and grind of the ocean that liberates salt and other sediment from the surrounding rocks. The average salinity of the oceans is around 35 grams of salt per liter of water (about 1 oz. in 61 cubic inches), the same balance as found in human blood. Salinity is greater in the tropics where the sun's heat evaporates the water. Meanwhile at the polar caps fresh water from the melting ice helps to dilute the mix.

Look out to sea and nothing is still. Ocean waters are in constant motion, driven by the gravitational pull of the moon and the prevailing winds which might push and draw waves from the world's shorelines. Nor has ocean science remained static.

For years there were just four recognized oceans in the world; the Atlantic, the Pacific, the Indian and the Arctic. Beyond the big four are smaller seas and gulfs extending from them. But recently specialist scientists were so uncomfortable with the traditional definition that they designated the waters surrounding Antarctica up to 60 degrees latitude as the Southern Ocean. For the first time a single ocean now encircled the Earth. The Southern Ocean is the fourth largest of the five oceans, being larger than the distant Arctic Ocean but smaller than the Pacific, Atlantic and Indian.

Combined, the world's oceans are thought to contain 1,340 million cubic kilometers (around 321 million cubic miles) of water. Almost half of this grand total is in the deepest parts of the oceans, about which the least is known. Intense water pressure, lack of light and an uncomfortably cold temperature stand in the way of extensive exploration. Technology is still playing catch-up as far as deep water expeditions are concerned.

It is certain, however, that the history of the world's seas parallels that of the land. Geologists have charted clues about the changing shape of the planet because 225 million years ago, rather than the five continents we have now, there was one giant continent surrounded by a single ocean. Despite the ensuing chasm of many hundreds of miles forged over millennia, the theme of geological trends can be identified and matched. For example, the rock strata of western Africa synchronize with the geological forms of eastern South America, indicating they were once linked. The shapes of today's continents are another clue. It is possible to see on a globe roughly how they once interlocked.

OCEAN LAYERS

On the surface the seas appear uniform for mile after long mile. Beneath, we see a different story with a range of environments that comprise a colossal and fluid ecosystem.

Scientifically speaking the open ocean is divided into five distinct layers or zones that are defined by the levels of light. They are called the sunlit, twilight, dark, abyssal and hadal zones and are known collectively as the pelagic zone. The word pelagic is derived from the Greek word for open sea. In addition, the shoreline forms a separate zone called the littoral zone, and the bottom of the sea comprises the benthic and demersal zones.

Each zone contains life forms specially adapted to live in those specific conditions. Of course, the deepest of the zones is the most challenging and there are far fewer creatures inhabiting this hostile environment than those closer to the surface. Sea-faring animals from the upper ocean zones risk being crushed by the pressure of the depths if they stray out of their preferred habitat. Likewise, deep sea marine creatures will be in peril if they rise towards the surface away from the intensely pressured existence they have evolved to tolerate.

As there is frictional stress existing between the zones it is possible for scientists to clearly define them. At the interface between two distinctive levels there are a range of phenomena in evidence, including the ability for sound to travel through specific lines of water.

This same friction also causes surface water in the northern hemisphere to travel at 90° to the right of the winds while in the southern hemisphere surface water goes 90° to the left of the winds.

As seawater gets colder it shrinks and becomes denser. At the same time the pressure increases. However, once it reaches minus 2.2°C (28°F) the process ends. The water is as cold and dense as it is ever going to get.

The sunlit zone

The surface of the ocean is the sunlit zone, hardly surprising as it is illuminated and warmed by the heat of the sun. Scientifically, it is known as the epipelagic layer.

Its depth extends to a maximum of about 200 m (656 ft) in the open ocean in areas that are tropical or sub tropical. In colder regions where the water is murkier the sunlit zone is much narrower and ends at just 100 m (328 ft). Technically, it depends on the quality of light within the ocean. It extends to the depth where light intensity is no less than one per cent of that at the surface. So in cold or stormy weather the number of cubic liters of water considered as part of the sunlit layer decreases dramatically.

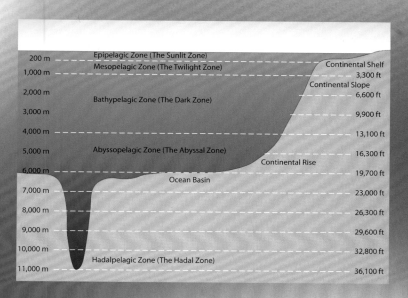

200 m	Epipelagic Zone (The Sunlit Zone)
1,000 m	Mesopelagic Zone (The Twilight Zone)
	Continental Shelf 3,300 ft
	Continental Slope
2,000 m	Bathypelagic Zone (The Dark Zone) 6,600 ft
3,000 m	9,900 ft
4,000 m	13,100 ft
5,000 m	Abyssopelagic Zone (The Abyssal Zone) 16,300 ft
	Continental Rise
6,000 m	19,700 ft
	Ocean Basin
7,000 m	23,000 ft
8,000 m	26,300 ft
9,000 m	29,600 ft
10,000 m	32,800 ft
	Hadalpelagic Zone (The Hadal Zone)
11,000 m	36,100 ft

▲ *The ocean has been categorized into five layers.*

The sunlit layer stays relatively stable in the tropics where solar energy keeps sea waters at around 25°C (77°F). However in the mid-latitudes surface waters, which can get as hot as those in the tropics during the summer, will fall to a much lower 10°C (50°F) in the winter so the sunlit zone has different seasonal sizes. Polar waters are much colder and sea water freezes at a few degrees below zero, depending on the saltiness.

In waters that filter the rays of the sun the vast majority of ocean life is to be found, thriving in benevolent surroundings. Life is often further improved for marine life thanks to the existence of the continental shelf at the same corresponding depths, covered with the protective debris of rocks, gravels and sands eroded from the land and sea bottom.

What might you expect to find in the sea's warm embrace? Fish, sharks, tuna, dolphins and jellyfish are among the resident population of the sunlit zone, which is home to 90 per cent of all marine life.

◀ *This whitetip reef shark (Triaenodon obesus) is typical of the residents of the Sunlit Zone with their camouflage darker on top and lighter underneath.*

At the root of the food chain lies the group of tiny organisms called plankton and all ocean life depends on it. Phytoplankton can only live in the sunlit zone as it needs specific levels of light for photosynthesis. But when phytoplankton and their bedfellows zooplankton gather en masse in what is known as 'blooms' they absorb so much sunlight that other life becomes at risk.

The twilight zone

In the twilight zone, a mere one per cent of natural light filters down from the surface. Crucially, with the rays so diluted, photosynthesis cannot take place and this restricts the opportunities for smaller creatures of the sea to find a suitable habitat. There is, however, enough light for some of the larger predators to hunt by.

Scientists call this the mesopelagic or mid-ocean layer and it will be found between 200 and 1,000 m down (656–3,281 ft).

Down here oxygen becomes scarce although there is a surprising array of marine life, including swordfish, cuttlefish, wolf eels and squid. There are also regular day-time visitors to the twilight zone, including the bigeye tuna. Satellites have tracked tuna like these sheltering in the depths during the dangerous daylight hours and returning to the sunlit zone to feast during the night.

Tuna and numerous others make the upwards trek because there is not much to eat in the twilight zone, save for the on-going showers of 'marine snow'. This is mostly organic detritus and includes dead creatures, strings of bacteria, natural polymers and waste material mixed up with a bit of sand and soot.

So large is the nightly journey from the twilight to the food-rich sunlit zone that it is best described as the single largest migration of life on Earth.

Generally, life forms at this depth have evolved special features to make themselves as inconspicuous as possible. Some have become wafer thin so they all but disappear if they face a

▲ *Basking sharks (Cetorhinus maximus) rise to the surface to feed but are commonly found to depths of 910 metres (2,990 ft).*

hunter. Others are almost translucent so they successfully merge into their surroundings. Still others have developed reflective surfaces to divert the light. One typical feature of all creatures in the twilight zone is large eyes, designed to make the most of what little light is available. At the lower depths of this zone bioluminescent creatures become apparent.

Fish living in the twilight zone like to maintain their body temperature and their very survival is at risk if they don't do so. It would be disastrous if they lost themselves in much colder water for long periods. Happily, at the rear end of the twilight zone there is a feature known as a thermocline which stops them doing just that. A thermocline is a layer within the ocean in which temperature changes swiftly, thus repelling heat-sensitive life forms. The thermocline is much smaller in waters that are uniformly cold, as in the polar regions.

◄ *The spotted ratfish (Hydrolagus colliei) is a common inhabitant of the mesopelagic zone where it preys on crabs, clams, shrimp, worms and smaller fish.*

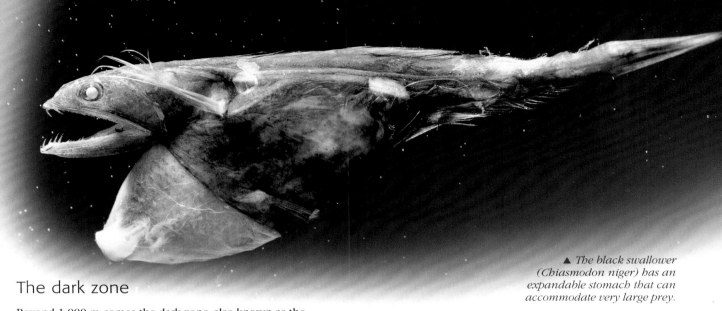

▲ *The black swallower (Chiasmodon niger) has an expandable stomach that can accommodate very large prey.*

The dark zone

Beyond 1,000 m comes the dark zone, also known as the bathypelagic zone or the deep water layer. It is pitch black here as no natural rays can penetrate this far down to either heat or light the water. In turn, that means most of the creatures found here are either blind or have developed bioluminescence – their own light source – from curious, light-emitting organs. Indeed, this is the only light that can penetrate the endless gloom.

The temperature of the water from here on down is consistently between 2 and 4°C (35–39°F).

Meanwhile water pressure is a colossal 403 bar (5,845 psi). Nonetheless, despite the grim conditions, there are examples of cunningly adapted marine creatures no doubt living happy, fulfilled lives. To do so they have liquid-filled bodies without cavities, such as lungs, that would be crushed by the pressure. Creatures living here use other gases in their swim bladders to control their movements, rather than oxygen, which is used by those living nearer the surface.

Leatherback turtles and elephant seals are known to dive into these obscure depths and sperm whales will also hunt for squid

here. There are other creatures, of course, far less familiar to us that can be found here. Thanks to the lack of light, most are either red or black in color.

No plants can live at this kind of depth so most of the living things rely again on marine snow, or what is left of it, coming down from the ocean surface. Failing that, they are compelled to eat their neighbors.

Here the ocean floor – or benthopelagic layer – is covered with thick sediment. This has built up over hundreds of millions of years and in some places can be more than 5 km (3 miles) deep. It is made of general debris like sand, gravel and stone washed from the continental shelf. A fine silt drifts slowly through the water until it lands here, as do rock particles from melting icebergs. In the mix there is also sediment which rejoices in the glorious name of biogenic ooze, the remains of long dead life forms.

▶ *The fangtooth (Anoplogaster cornuta) is more commonly found at depths of 200-2,000 m (660-6,560 ft) but have been found as deep as 5,000 m (16,400 ft).*

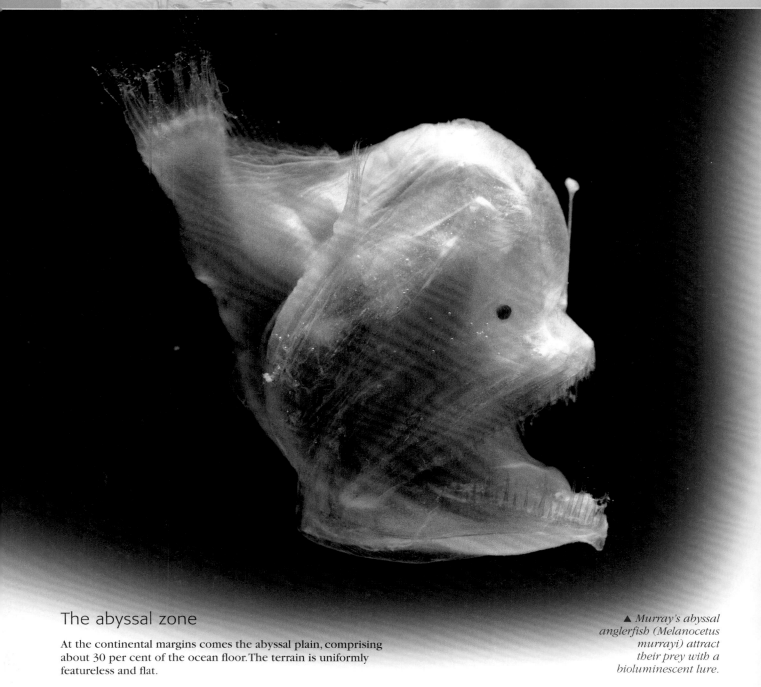

The abyssal zone

At the continental margins comes the abyssal plain, comprising about 30 per cent of the ocean floor. The terrain is uniformly featureless and flat.

▲ *Murray's abyssal anglerfish (Melanocetus murrayi) attract their prey with a bioluminescent lure.*

Characteristic of the sea bed in this deep ocean zone are potato-sized manganese nodules which contain a variety of valuable minerals, including titanium and barium as well as manganese. They were first discovered in 1803 but so far have proved too difficult to retrieve for exploitation of their mineral content. Each nodule has formed over millions of years around a fragment of solid debris such as a tiny fossil and is then surrounded by concentric layers of iron and manganese. Their diameter can range from microscopic up to 10 cm (4 in).

Typically animals living in the abyssal zone are blind, sluggish in movement and slow growing. The lack of food means these hardy creatures have to conserve their energy. So they wait for prey to swim by rather than embark on hunting expeditions. They have long, needle -sharp teeth and jaws that can unhinge to swallow prey larger than themselves. Predators such as flashlight fish use bioluminescent lures, light generated by a chemical reaction, to attract their prey. Others simply lie in wait waiting for an unsuspecting passerby.

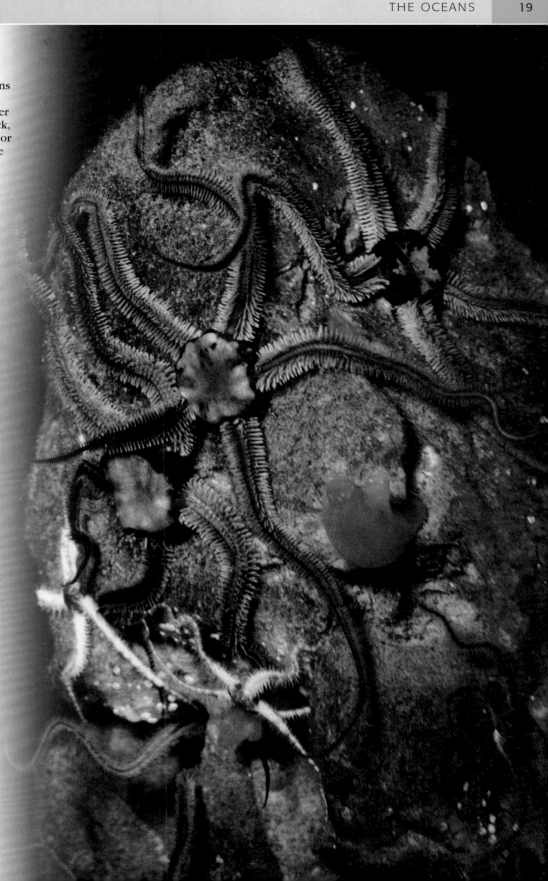

The hadal zone

The fractured ocean floor contains mighty fissures, created by the movement of the plates that cover the earth's surface. Obsidian black, these features are called abysses or ocean trenches and comprise the hadal zone. Although the water temperature remains an even 2°C (36°F) the water pressure is immense.

Not many species can live in such an inhospitable environment but the few that do are there in numbers. Mostly they are invertebrates like worms, tiny squids, shrimps, crustaceans like the sea spider and brittlestars. There are a few fish – perhaps more than we know about. It is conceivable that many species survive outside the boundaries of our knowledge in the hadal zone.

The deepest known point in the ocean is located in the Mariana Trench off the coast of Japan at 10,911 m (35,797 ft). The temperature of the water remains just above freezing but the pressure is an incredible 1103 bar (15,997 psi).

▶ *Brittlestars are one of the few species that are known to inhabit the deepest depths of the oceans.*

WATER PRESSURE AND TEMPERATURE

We humans are perfectly adapted to life on the land, where we are not even aware of the air pressure around us. Splashing about in the shallows it is difficult to spot the difference. But cast us below the water and suddenly the pressure begins to tell.

Water pressure, also known as hydrostatic pressure, is measured in bars. At sea level it amounts to one 'atmospheric bar' 14.5 psi. Pressure increases by one bar with every 10 m (33 ft) of depth.

▶ *NASA uses satellites to provide composite images of temperature (blue is cold while red indicates the hottest) of the Earth's oceans*

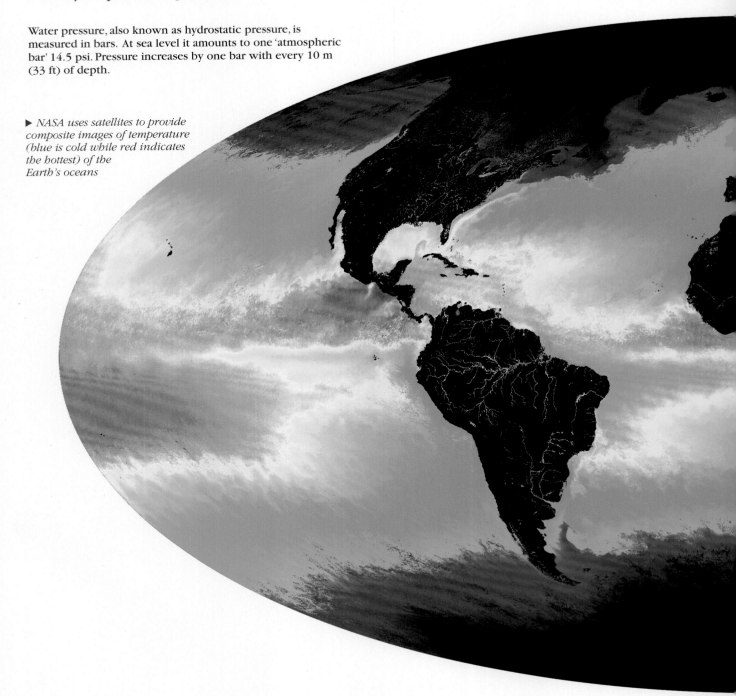

If you could hold your breath and dive down 10 m your lungs would contract to half their normal size, refilling only when you returned to the water's surface. Using a different illustration, if you dived underwater holding a bag of air it would halve in size after every 10 m.

To dive to these depths, you would need the oxygen tanks associated with SCUBA diving rigs. When you breathe from the tanks the air is pressurized, matching the hydrostatic pressure of the water; it has to be or it wouldn't come out of the tank.

Thus pressure builds in the deep. The wreck of the RMS Titanic – sitting at 3,797m (12,460 ft) below the north Atlantic is subject to pressure of around 448 bar (6,497 psi), making it remote to explorers. Most of the creatures that live in these depths have adapted to endure the pressure. They have bodies of uncrushable gelatin and cartilage rather than bones, and lack collapsible cavities, such as lungs, which would be too fragile to withstand pressures such as this.

Water temperature at surface level varies according to the season and even whether it is night or day. At depth, however, it will sink no lower than 2°C (35.6°F). It plummets to that baseline soon after the bottom of the sunlit zone is reached.

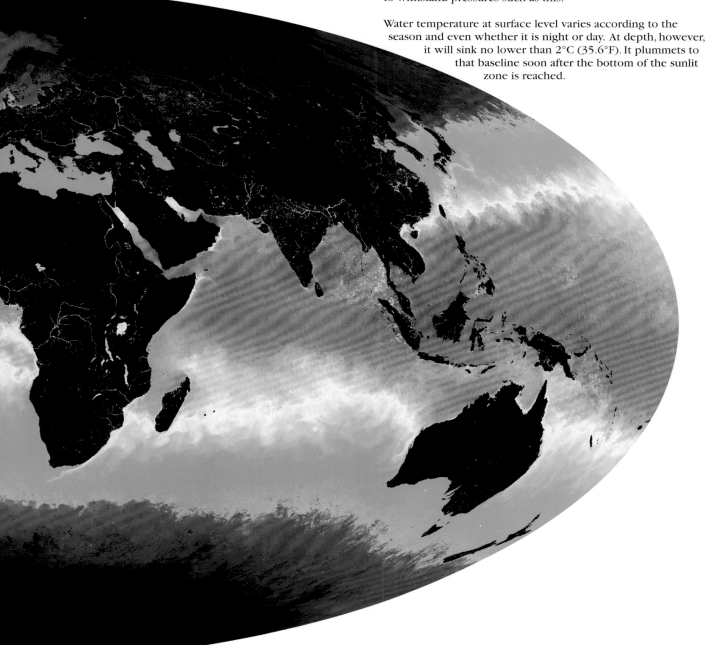

EFFECTS OF WINDS OVER THE OCEAN

Sea-faring explorers from centuries past took to the oceans to discover what lay beyond the immediate horizon. The ships they sailed in were often little more than leaky tubs. But, thanks to the winds over the sea, they covered extraordinary distances and discovered new civilizations and virgin territories. For it is out to sea, where there are no obstacles in their path, that the winds blow the strongest and the longest.

Wind is created by the effect of the sun's heat and the earth's rotation. In general terms, it can be divided into three global circulatory systems or cells. Beginning at the equator, the Hadley cells swing into action as warm air rises from the equator to cool in the higher atmosphere before descending at around 30° N and 30°S and feeding back to the starting

▲ *Wind power is still a popular method of ocean travel in the 21st Century.*

point. The system is named for George Hadley, an English barrister, who wrote 'On the cause of the general trade winds' back in 1735. It was a century before people realized he was largely right.

In the colder climes of the Arctic and Antarctic, polar cells collect air descending towards the poles and dispatch it in the direction of the equator. Between the two lie the Ferrel cells which function at sub polar latitudes and are dependent on the other cell systems for their existence. The Ferrel cell system was defined following work by American meteorologist William Ferrel during the 19th century.

As the earth spins the movement of the cells is distorted. This creates what is known as the Coriolis force. The way the air is deflected is directly related to both the latitude and the speed at which the air is moving. Slow-blowing winds will be dented only a small amount while the path of stronger winds is more profoundly affected. Winds blowing close to the poles will be deflected more than similar winds at the equator because the earth has a smaller diameter there. The Coriolis force only acts on large objects moving considerable distances. A ship at sea is too small to feel its effect.

Of course, those hapless sailors in centuries gone by knew nothing of this. However, they were intimately acquainted with the effects of this highbrow science. For winds like the Roaring Forties could whip up waves to hazardous heights. Indeed, freak waves have been known to swamp entire ships, with the loss of all hands. Around the equator the trade winds blow so hard and constantly the waters there are more than 30 cm (1 ft) higher than elsewhere.

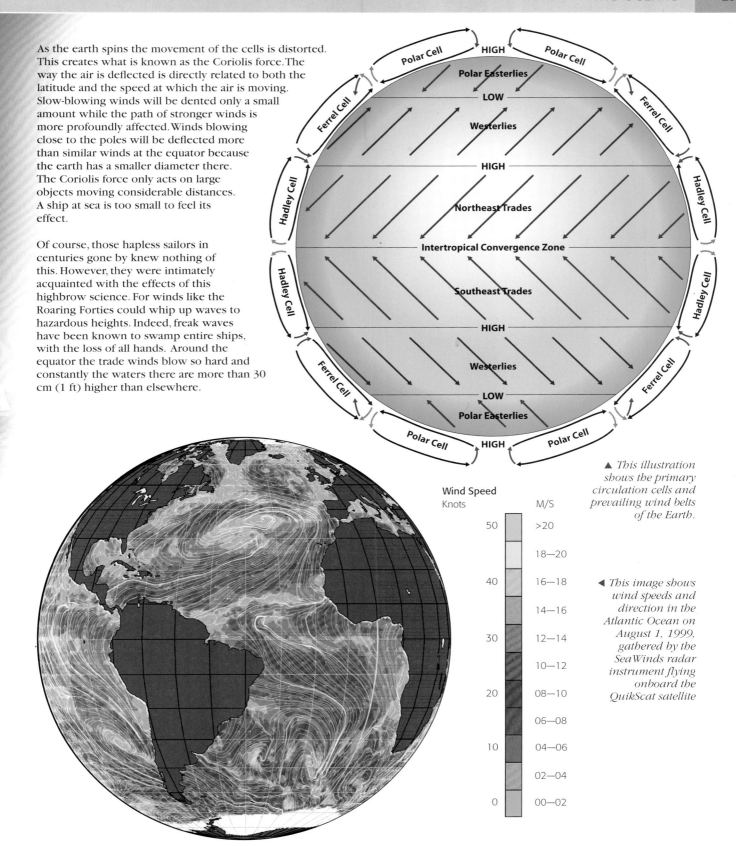

▲ *This illustration shows the primary circulation cells and prevailing wind belts of the Earth.*

◀ *This image shows wind speeds and direction in the Atlantic Ocean on August 1, 1999, gathered by the SeaWinds radar instrument flying onboard the QuikScat satellite*

Wind Speed

Knots	M/S
50	>20
	18—20
40	16—18
	14—16
30	12—14
	10—12
20	08—10
	06—08
10	04—06
	02—04
0	00—02

When a strong wind blows over the ocean some water on the windward side is lowered while some of the water on the leeward side is raised. How much water is displaced depends on the strength of the wind, how long it blows for and the amount of water involved. And that's the technical explanation for the creation of a wave.

Curiously, wind helps to support abundant ocean life; when the easterly trade winds of the tropics drag water away from the equator they spark an upwelling, as cold, dense water from the deep shoots up to the warmer, shallow surface, dramatically lowering the temperature. This water is rich in nutrients and it supports ample fish stocks.

But as natures gives, she can also take away. If the pressure that drives the easterly trade winds falters and dies, warmer waters spread across the Pacific. This creates a thermocline, a blanket that spreads between the warm waters of the sunlit zone and the depths, which sinks and in doing so smothers the upwelling. This natural phenomena, called the El Nino effect, results in a reduction in food available for sea creatures and the knock-on effect is to reduce the number of fish, creating shortages and crippling the fishing industry. Beyond that, the poultry industry also feels the pinch as fish waste, which is normally turned into chicken food, rises in price.

◄ The wind has the power to turn a calm sea into stormy waves.

▼ The exposed vertebrae of this blue whale (Balaenoptera musculus) is a clear indication of malnourishment due to the previous year's El Nino.

▲ While sailors had to learn the patterns of marine winds, nautical charts were invaluable on their journeys of exploration.

SOUND THROUGH WATER

The romance of hearing whales whistling or dolphins chatter through the water is ceaselessly enchanting to the ears of man. For marine creatures, however, the phenomenon of sound travelling through water has a far more practical purpose and that is to locate and hunt down prey. And for humans there is a somewhat sinister use for it too, being key in submarine warfare.

Sound travels four times faster through the water than it does through the air, achieving a speed of around 1,500 m (5,000 ft) per second. It also spreads much further because there is little to stand in its way. It can bounce off the ocean bottom or its surface.

In rough seas sound does not travel as far as it would in calm waters while winds across the ocean 's surface tend to scatter and disrupt sound quality.

But there is one place in the ocean where, thanks to optimum conditions, sounds will reach out for miles. It is known as the Sound Fixing and Ranging channel and it occurs where the combination of pressure, temperature and, to a lesser extent, salinity is ideally suited to carrying sound. Researchers believe it is this channel that provides humpback whales with an ability to communicate over many miles of open ocean. For their part, marine scientists use hydrophones – a kind of underwater microphone – to monitor sea-faring creatures

like dolphins and whales. The device, pioneered during the First World War to combat submarines, also offers invaluable information about the distribution of marine life, the size of animals, their movements and their behavior.

Areas of water where transmission of sound is poor are known as shadow zones, while high intensity areas are called caustic zones. In addition there are convergence zones, where sound generated near the surface bounces off the ocean bed and then reflects back from the surface.

The water cycle

Our oceans are replenished by rivers and rain. This is all part of a cycle that keeps the earth's waters on the move continuously, driven by the heat of the sun.

The water cycle – or hydrologic cycle as it is properly known – has no beginning and no end. Although it can appear elaborate, it is in fact beautifully simple. Let's start the explanation at the top, with the water particles

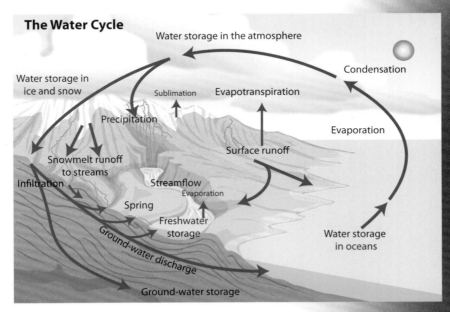

The Water Cycle

Water storage in the atmosphere

Condensation

Water storage in ice and snow

Sublimation

Evapotranspiration

Precipitation

Evaporation

Surface runoff

Snowmelt runoff to streams

Infiltration

Streamflow

Evaporation

Spring

Freshwater storage

Water storage in oceans

Ground-water discharge

Ground-water storage

▲ *This illustration shows how water is recycled in a continuous manner.*

▶ *The 'song' sung by male humpback whales can last up to 20 minutes and be repeated for hours.*

hanging high in earth's atmosphere. As the particles cool they form into clouds and are soon on the move in the grip of global winds. Eventually precipitation in the form of rain, hail or snow from these clouds begins.

Some of this precipitation falls into lakes, rivers or the ocean. The remainder soaks into the land, where it may either be absorbed by the soil to be recycled through vegetation, or seep into underground stores of groundwater. Perhaps years later, it might emerge in a spring.

Snow that falls on high ground can be trapped by the ice for hundreds of years. But if it melts it will join the trickles or torrents from the mountains tumbling down to lakes or to the sea. It joins the rain that went directly into the sea to be stored there until evaporation dispatches it back into the atmosphere as water vapor. Rising air currents take it skywards in the

form of particles. Soon cooler temperatures will fashion it into clouds and the process begins again.

While ocean water is drawn up as vapor as part of the water cycle, atmospheric water is fresh rather than salty. This is because seawater leaves behind its salt content during evaporation. That is how vast salt pans have formed in East Africa and North America. Sometimes there are crusts of salt visible along a shore line too.

THE OCEAN'S FOOD CHAIN

While the commonly used term is food chain, it is perhaps best considered as a web as the diet of marine creatures isn't restricted size-wise to their nearest neighbor.

Starting at the bottom, there's one all important anchor. It is the plant-like plankton which is tiny but nonetheless essential for all that. It is these minute specks that perform the miracle of photosynthesis. In short, they transform carbon dioxide and water into oxygen and energy-giving fodder. Having made their own food, they become tasty snacks for the larger zooplankton.

These are eaten by the next in line, the krill, who themselves are consumed by marine worms. The process goes on until the biggest marine creatures, like the dolphins and whales, are involved. But some larger fish eat not only the creatures that feast on zooplankton but zooplankton themselves. So there is nothing so convenient as a straight line in the marine food chain, more a maze of different and often interconnecting corridors.

This is how energy is transferred up the line, from plant-eating plankton, known as phytoplankton, to porpoise. But the system is (largely) inefficient with predators having to consume ten of its prey to garner the same (amount of) energy. So with each new level fewer creatures can be supported. Thus the food chain now seems more like a pyramid with countless phytoplankton at its base and a few alpha hunters at its pinnacle. However, because of the vital role of the phytoplankton, it is clear the sun plays the same crucial role in driving the food chain in the sea as it does on land.

▶ *Caribbean reef sharks (Carcharhinus perezii) stir up sand in a feeding frenzy, Bahamas*

▼ *In similar circumstances to the water cycle, the marine food chain is a never-ending circle of nutrition.*

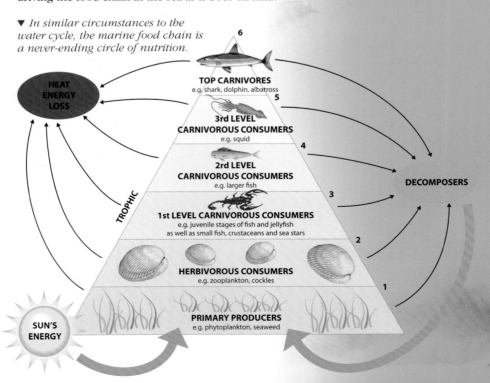

HEAT ENERGY LOSS

6

TOP CARNIVORES
e.g. shark, dolphin, albatross

5

3rd LEVEL CARNIVOROUS CONSUMERS
e.g. squid

4

2nd LEVEL CARNIVOROUS CONSUMERS
e.g. larger fish

3

1st LEVEL CARNIVOROUS CONSUMERS
e.g. juvenile stages of fish and jellyfish as well as small fish, crustaceans and sea stars

2

HERBIVOROUS CONSUMERS
e.g. zooplankton, cockles

1

PRIMARY PRODUCERS
e.g. phytoplankton, seaweed

TROPHIC

DECOMPOSERS

SUN'S ENERGY

SEAWEED AND ALGAE

For such an apparently simple structure, seaweeds present scientists and biologists with a problem. Green seaweeds are a type of algae and belong to the plant kingdom. But red and brown seaweeds, although also a type of algae, do not have roots or flowers or stems and are not considered by all experts to be true plants.

Some seaweeds are annuals and complete their lifecycle within a year while others are perennial and can live for many seasons. Furthermore, some seaweeds are parasitic, living off fellow species. Primitive though they appear, there is nothing straightforward about our seaweeds.

▼ *A pineapple sea cucumber crawls through algae in Papua New Guinea's Kimbe Bay.*

▲ *In the right conditions, eroded boulders such as these off the coast of Norfolk soon become covered in algae.*

With photosynthesis, seaweeds can turn solar energy into calories and thus they provide food containing a rich source of minerals for many marine creatures. In addition, a canopy of seaweed forms an important habitat that offers protection and camouflage to smaller marine creatures. Drifting seaweed is thought to partially explain the distribution of species from island to island, as marine life can hitch a ride on it over long distances.

Although similar in basic structure to terrestrial plants, seaweed does not have roots. Instead it depends on a 'holdfast' so it can attach itself to rocks or the sea bed. Some – but not all – seaweed have a stipe or type of stem. Others grow into a thallus, with flattened leaf-like blades. Together stipe and blade are known as a frond. Thanks to gas-filled bladders, many seaweeds can float to the ocean's surface which is the ideal spot for photosynthesis to occur.

Algae

A primordial organism that was probably among the first to appear in the ocean, algae depends on the sun for its existence. Accordingly it grows only in a layer on the surface of the ocean that descends to no more than 30 m (100 ft).

Too small to be seen without a microscope, green algae are mostly single celled and fall into the marine class of phytoplankton. Only in spring when there is a sudden increase in light and warmth does the existence of green algae become apparent in the form of a bloom which will turn an ocean green and murky. Zooplankton are the main beneficiaries when this happens as their food supply is consequently abundant.

Green seaweed

When green algae become visible to the naked eye it is known as green seaweed. Unlike other plants that need roots to supply nutrients and gases, green seaweeds absorb food from the environment.

There are about 1,200 different species of green seaweed and they can be found world-wide. In temperate and cold waters they grow on rocks, in rock pools and around the shore line. In tropical waters they live in shallow lagoons and on rocks as well as along the sandy sea bed. Although they have no roots or stems, they come in a huge range of shapes and sizes. Green seaweeds can be thread-like, in ribbons, in tubes or fans or more.

Red and brown seaweeds

Red and brown seaweeds live in fast-flowing waters around the sea shore or on the sea bed. To a casual observer they may look similar, but red and brown seaweeds are considered separately by marine botanists because they have different pigments for photosynthesis.

In size they vary from tiny single cell structures to giant kelp that sways impressively in fast-flowing currents after achieving lengths of 100 m (328 ft) or more. They reproduce in two ways, either sexually through spores or asexually by division and fragmentation.

There are about 5,500 different species of red seaweeds, ranging in color from coral pink to reddish black. A red protein called phycoerythrin is responsible for the seaweeds' color. There is also a substance that absorbs blue light and that allows them to survive in deeper, darker waters than brown seaweed. Perhaps because of this, they are much less common in tropical waters.

Many red seaweeds have a two-stage life cycle. Initially they have upstanding filaments, ideal for when the water is calm. As the season turns, so the red seaweeds develop a crusty, creeping frond which is better able to withstand rougher seas and stronger currents.

Types of brown seaweed are frequently left exposed to the ravages of sunlight because they live within tidal drags. Rather than dry to a crisp, some species contain moisture-retaining tissues and cells that remain full of sea water. Others cover themselves in mucus so they do not dry out nor are they an attractive food source for passing animals.

Giant kelp forests

Giant kelp is one of the fastest growing and largest plants in the world. Like the equatorial rain forest to which they bear a passing resemblance, the giant kelp forests that exist out of public gaze are among the most important ecosystems on the planet.

This striking form of marine algae tends to grow best in areas of upwelling where the waters are cool and nutrient rich, although there are limited examples of kelp in deep tropical waters. In the right conditions giant kelp can grow vertically up to an astonishing 60 cm (24 in) a day in spring and summer – making it one of the fastest sprinters of the plant world.

Beneath its canopy the kelp forest shields a thriving community, existing in different strata. Like the tropical rain forests there is a sunlit upper level, a twilight middle storey and a dark floor. Some species use it for shelter, others for food. Still more are drawn to kelp forests to hunt among the fronds for their supper.

Different kelp species live alongside one another in the forests. They are upstanding in the water thanks to the gas-filled bladders located usually between stipe and frond (stalk and leaf).

And, like its terrestrial equivalent, the kelp forests are in jeopardy. Sea urchins are the dominant herbivore and it is these spiny menaces who will decimate the kelp forest if left unchecked by predators. Overfishing has affected the balance between predator and prey in the oceans and kelp forests are likely to be over-grazed because of it.

A heavy storm can also wreak havoc in a kelp forest but it is usually only the upper layer that is at risk.

◄ *Furbellows – the largest European seaweed, growing up to 5 m in length in a matter of months – amongst red seaweeds.*

▶ *Sunlight shining through a forest of Giant Kelp.*

THE OCEANIC CRUST AND UNDERWATER VOLCANOES

There are more than 5,000 active volcanoes shielded by the waves, unseen by the world's population who rarely spare a thought for the geo-thermal activity brewing up beneath the ocean floor. But these firecrackers are important and, without realizing it, we feel the effects of them on a daily basis.

When underwater volcanoes erupt the lava heats the water. As this vast amount of thermal heating rises to the surface of the ocean, it creates high velocity winds that in turn drive the earth's weather patterns.

Thanks to the constant movement of the tectonic plates, no part of the ocean floor is older than about 180 million years. While that sounds like a great age, the continental rocks that make up dry land are more than twice as ancient.

The oceanic crust is made up of various heavy basaltic lavas and related igneous rocks, to a depth of between 6 and 8 km (4–6 miles), and forms more than two thirds of the earth's

▶ *Surtsey, off the southern coast of Iceland, was formed in a volcanic eruption which began 130 meters (426 ft) below sea level and reached the surface on November 14, 1963*

surface. These rocks are heavier and denser than those of the continental crust and only infrequently break through to the surface – Iceland is a rare example.

The relative youth of the oceanic crust is because it constantly renews itself from the underlying molten mantle. As it erupts through fissures and cracks in the ocean bed a new crust is spewed forth.

▶ *Sangean Island is an active volcano towering 1,800 meters (5,905 ft) above the tranquil waters of the Indian Ocean.*

▼ *The summit of West Mata Volcano in the Samoas, shown in red, is nearly a mile below the ocean surface.*

(Meters) **Depth** (Miles)

1165	3800 ft
1500	1 mile
1800	
2100	
2400	
2700	
3000	2 miles

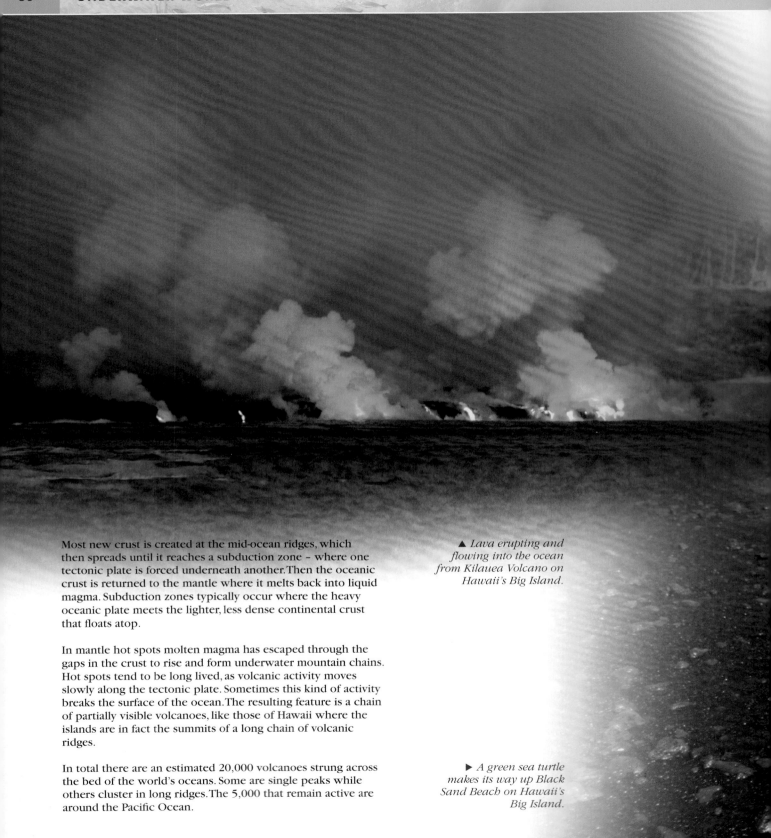

Most new crust is created at the mid-ocean ridges, which then spreads until it reaches a subduction zone – where one tectonic plate is forced underneath another. Then the oceanic crust is returned to the mantle where it melts back into liquid magma. Subduction zones typically occur where the heavy oceanic plate meets the lighter, less dense continental crust that floats atop.

In mantle hot spots molten magma has escaped through the gaps in the crust to rise and form underwater mountain chains. Hot spots tend to be long lived, as volcanic activity moves slowly along the tectonic plate. Sometimes this kind of activity breaks the surface of the ocean. The resulting feature is a chain of partially visible volcanoes, like those of Hawaii where the islands are in fact the summits of a long chain of volcanic ridges.

In total there are an estimated 20,000 volcanoes strung across the bed of the world's oceans. Some are single peaks while others cluster in long ridges. The 5,000 that remain active are around the Pacific Ocean.

▲ *Lava erupting and flowing into the ocean from Kilauea Volcano on Hawaii's Big Island.*

▶ *A green sea turtle makes its way up Black Sand Beach on Hawaii's Big Island.*

Unlike their dry land counterparts, live deep water volcanoes do not hiss with steam and gases. The tremendous pressure of water bearing down on them prevents it from happening. Lava still erupts though, spreading across the sea floor and cooling so rapidly that it shatters into sand and rubble. The debris that results on the ocean bed is soon swept far and wide by the ocean currents.

Volcanoes that erupt in middling depths spew lava that cools into a solid crust around its hotter core, creating what's known as pillow lava.

When sea water pours into an active, shallow submarine vent the resulting eruption throws out steam and molten rock which can turn into volcanic glass. The black sands of Hawaii were created by the violence that occurred when sea water and hot lava united.

The Mid-Atlantic Ridge was created by oceanic plate divergence, which means the plates were moving away from each other. Features including the Pacific Rim of Fire were caused by ocean plate convergence, when the plates moved towards one another.

Another associated deep water feature are seamounts, which are isolated, extinct volcanoes that rise abruptly from a depth of about 4,000 m (13,123 ft) to stand about 1,000 m (3,281 ft) in height. There are an estimated 30,000 seamounts scattered across the oceans.

UNDERWATER CAVES

Sea caves that punctuate the foot of cliffs are hollow monuments to the power of the pounding waves. Exposed coastlines are especially vulnerable as strong winds whip up waves that are armed with sand, pebbles and other beach detritus, before hurling them at the cliff face.

▲ *Galapagos sea lions play in cave where they escape the heat of the day.*

The target cliff must bear a weakness, like a fault between layers of rock or a seam of softer stone, before serious cave-style erosion begins. Wave action will attack the entire cliff face uniformly until it happens across a flaw. Then each roller will play its part in sculpting a single chamber or passage.

Thereafter the hydraulic power of the waves forces compressed air into any small crevices and cracks. As the air re-expands it creates a tremendous force within the confined area that ruptures the rocks, helping to speed up the process.

Caves that have a jagged outline and are irregular in shape are probably reflecting the lines of weakness in the rock face. Those that are round with smooth walls and a pebble-lined floor are more likely to have been thrashed by the circular motion of the stones as they are swirled by the surf around the cave.

On exposed headlands wave refraction focuses the sea's energy into the rocks, in time cutting away indentations and deep cavities in the base of the cliffs that develop into sea caves. Once such a weakness is created the process can only continue. In time such caves on either side of the headland will succumb to wave action, deepening and widening until a tunnel is cut right through the cliff to form an arch. Years later the arch will collapse and what was once a headland will be left as an isolated stack of stone.

Many sea caves are partially or fully exposed at low tide but fill as the sea flows in again. The vertical and overhanging walls of the caves provide a safer environment for many marine invertebrates, who are out of the path of roving crabs, sea urchins or starfish. Predators like this are easily washed off the sheer rocks by waves.

Usually caves are bare of seaweed. They are rarely penetrated by sunlight so the growing conditions are far from perfect. Moreover their spores are soon flushed out of caves by the sea before they have an opportunity to establish themselves. Conditions inside caves can change, however. Some have been deserted by the waves after a change in the path of the sea. Caves on the Norwegian coast, for example, are some 30 m (98 ft) above sea level.

Invariably the largest sea caves face the prevailing seas. Accordingly they are to be found in the Shetland Islands, around Hawaii and along the west coast of the United States. Long held as places of romance and mystery, caves have often been celebrated in song and poetry. Fingal's Cave on the island of Staffa in the Inner Hebrides off Scotland is an impressive 70 m (230 ft) long with basalt columns which lend it the feel of a cathedral. With this in mind, it became the subject of an overture written by Felix Mendelssohn in the 19th century, when it was also featured in paintings and poems. In Capri, the Blue Grotto, named for the quality of its light, draws tourists by the thousand. The Romans were so taken with it that they built a tunnel and stairway for easy access.

OCEANS OF THE WORLD

Nowhere do the world's oceans look more magnificent than from the far-off perspective of space. The first astronauts marveled at how the earth looked like a wreathed blue pearl, with the oceans dominant. The most famous picture of earth taken from space was captured by the crew of Apollo 17 in 1972, impressing on the public perhaps for the first time the scale of the planet's oceans.

Hardly surprising, then, that an entire army of marine biologists, re-enforced by ranks of other scientists, has often had to admit defeat when it comes to unravelling the secrets of the seas. The sheer vastness of the oceans has turned out to be a pretty impenetrable defense system.

Consider for a moment the depths to which science must travel to reap the necessary knowledge about ocean life. The Arctic Ocean is the shallowest of the big five, with an average depth of 1,038 m (3,406 ft). Depth-wise the Indian Ocean averages out at 3,886 m (12,750 ft), the Atlantic 3,658 m (12,000 ft) and the Pacific 3,962 m (13,000 ft). The Southern Ocean tops the lot with an average depth of between 4,000 and 5,000 m (13,123 ft to 16,404 ft).

Crucially, water is constantly on the move, recycling between the shallows and the depths, although it might take more than 200 years for water that sinks in the Arctic to resurface at the equator. It happens in several ways.

To begin with, there are two types of ocean current. Surface currents occur in the top layer, to a depth of 400 m (1,312 ft) and are largely driven by the wind. Deep water currents move more slowly and are shifted by gravity and density that are in turn governed by salinity and temperature.

Already we know that the world's oceans are steered by the Coriolis effect – which moves objects in the northern hemisphere to the right and objects in the southern hemisphere to the left – as well as gravity, wind and the heat of the sun. Together, the Coriolis effect and gravity produce the geostrophic current which travels horizontally through the ocean's upper layer.

But the biggest engine to power the world's seas on their ceaseless journey is the thermohaline conveyor belt, which snakes around the globe affecting everything from carbon dioxide levels, to the thickness of ice at the polar caps and the world-wide weather.

It is simplest to think of its starting point in the North Atlantic where cooling, salty, dense water sinks in such huge volumes in an action that has been likened to that of a plunger, pushing water around the rest of the world. These vast volumes of water descend to a great depth before circulating southwards down to the South Atlantic and racing around the Antarctic in the circumpolar current. There the conveyor belt is recharged with more cold, dense, salty water formed under the great ice shelves of Antarctica.

Now it heads for the equator before splitting to replenish the waters of both the Indian Ocean and the Pacific Ocean. The conveyor belt then travels north, gradually warming and rising en route to the North Pacific, then the South Atlantic and then the North Atlantic.

There are also five major gyres, currents that are pushed on by the Coriolis effect with a little help from the wind, and which are discussed later in the book.

The changes on the ocean's currents has a profound effect on the world's weather, and weather systems in turn effect the movement of the currents.

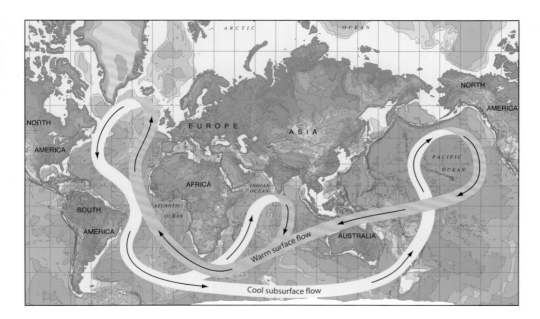

Warm surface flow

Cool subsurface flow

◄ *The thermohaline conveyor circulation is sometimes called the ocean conveyor belt, the great ocean conveyor, or the global conveyor belt.*

► *A view of the Earth from space, centering on the Indian Ocean.*

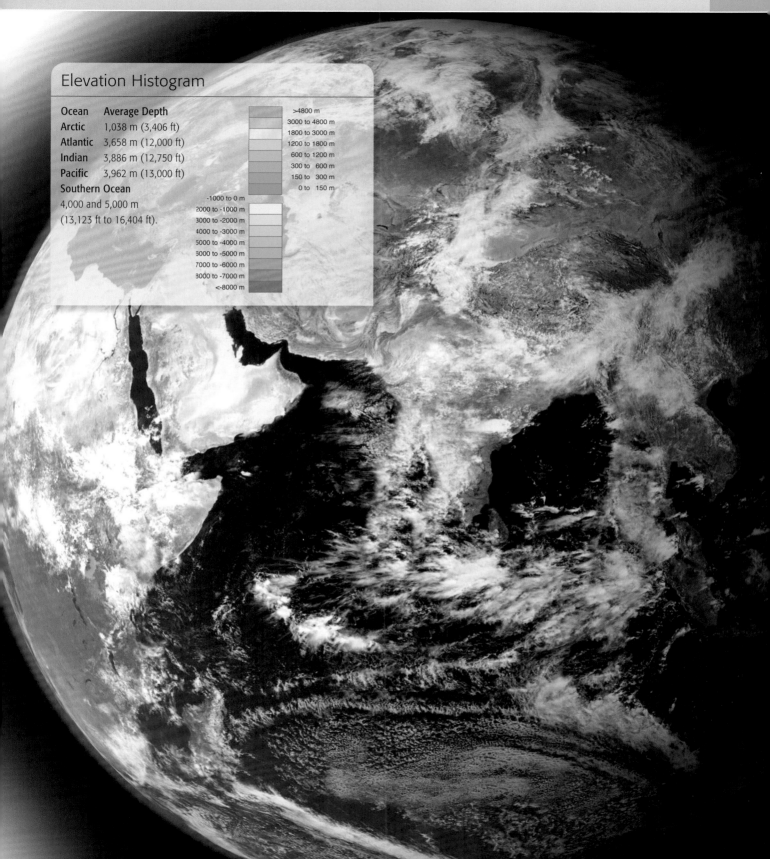

Elevation Histogram

Ocean	Average Depth
Arctic	1,038 m (3,406 ft)
Atlantic	3,658 m (12,000 ft)
Indian	3,886 m (12,750 ft)
Pacific	3,962 m (13,000 ft)
Southern Ocean	

4,000 and 5,000 m
(13,123 ft to 16,404 ft).

>4800 m
3000 to 4800 m
1800 to 3000 m
1200 to 1800 m
600 to 1200 m
300 to 600 m
150 to 300 m
0 to 150 m

-1000 to 0 m
2000 to -1000 m
3000 to -2000 m
4000 to -3000 m
5000 to -4000 m
6000 to -5000 m
7000 to -6000 m
8000 to -7000 m
<-8000 m

PACIFIC OCEAN

Largest by far of the bodies of water on Earth is the Pacific Ocean. It lies between continental North and South America in the east and Australasia and Asia in the west and stretches from the Arctic in the north to the Southern Ocean.

It was named *Mare Pacificum* or the Peaceful Sea by the Portuguese explorer Ferdinand Magellan, the leader of the first expedition to circumnavigate the globe. Magellan was killed during a battle in the Philippines before completing the voyage, and presumably before witnessing any Pacific typhoons, as peaceful is only partially accurate as a description of the ocean.

More than a quarter of the globe is covered by the Pacific Ocean and half the world's water lies within it. Still, it is not the ocean it used to be. Until 2000 its vital statistics were considerably larger until some of its waters were allocated to the newly recognized Southern Ocean. Moreover, also less obviously, the Pacific is shrinking while the Atlantic and the Indian Oceans are expanding, although the ground they are making is comparatively small. The Pacific Ocean is notionally divided by the equator into the North Pacific Ocean and the South Pacific Ocean. At the equator it measures 17,703 km (11,000 miles) across.

Its waters are breached by some 25,000 islands, more than in the rest of the oceans put together, often found in arcs or clusters. They come in four different types: coral reefs, uplifted coral platforms, continental islands such as New Guinea which was once part of Australia, and high islands, created by volcanic activity. The majority of Pacific islands lie in the South Pacific Ocean where a vast number are tiny and uninhabited.

The Pacific Ocean bed

The Pacific Ocean is still a very dynamic geological area with frequent earthquakes and volcanic activity. Beneath three quarters of it lies the Pacific Plate, one of the world's eight largest tectonic plates which is far from settled. In the south east it meets the Nazca Plate and the join forms the East Pacific Rise, a prominent mid-ocean ridge. In the western Pacific it meets the continental Eurasian Plate in addition to a number of smaller plates creating a vast subduction zone.

The Ring or Rim of Fire is a volatile 40,000 km (25,000 mile) long zone that encircles the Pacific Ocean and includes some of the most seismically lively parts of the planet. The unstable tectonics along the ring produce some 90 per cent of the world's earthquakes as well as most of its volcanic eruptions. Another feature of the Pacific bed are trenches and 18 of the worlds 22 major deep abysses are to be found here. The

▼ *The bed of the Pacific can be full of hidden surprises, such as this feathertail sting ray in Micronesia.*

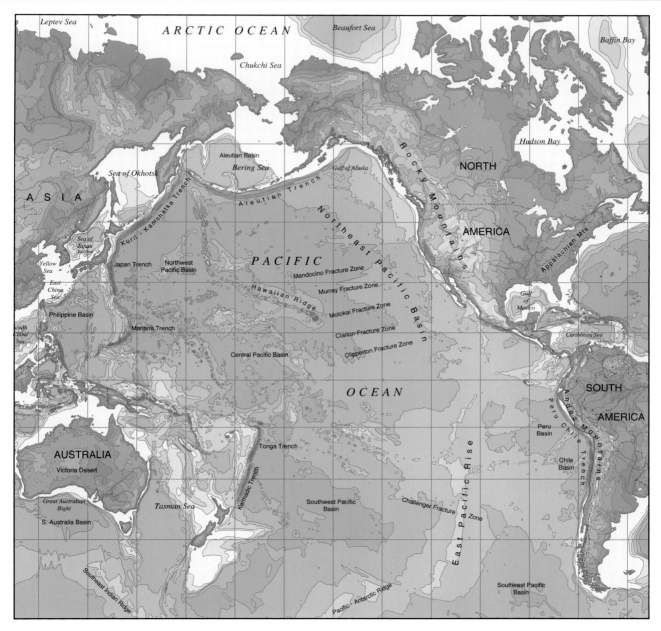

ARCTIC OCEAN

Leptev Sea
Beaufort Sea
Baffin Bay
Chukchi Sea

Sea of Okhotsk
Aleutian Basin
Bering Sea
Gulf of Alaska
Hudson Bay
NORTH
ASIA
AMERICA

Sea of Japan (East Sea)
Yellow Sea
Japan Trench
Northwest Pacific Basin
PACIFIC
Mendocino Fracture Zone
East China Sea
Murray Fracture Zone
Molokai Fracture Zone
Clarion Fracture Zone
Gulf of Mexico
Philippine Basin
Clipperton Fracture Zone
Caribbean Sea
South China Sea
Mariana Trench
Central Pacific Basin
OCEAN
SOUTH
AMERICA
Peru Basin
AUSTRALIA
Victoria Desert
Tonga Trench
Chile Basin
Great Australian Bight
Tasman Sea
Southwest Pacific Basin
Challenger Fracture Zone
S. Australia Basin
Southeast Pacific Basin
Southeast Indian Ridge
Pacific-Antarctic Ridge

▲ *This map shows the geographic features of the Pacific Ocean, the largest body of water on Earth.*

longest is the Central Pacific Trough that runs from Antarctica to the Aleutian Islands and then north to Japan and the west cost of America.

The deepest, the Mariana Trench, which runs for some 2,542 km (1,580 miles) north to south, was created by subduction, when two tectonic plates collided and one overwhelmed the other. Its deepest point is called Challenger Deep, for the British survey ship Challenger II which discovered it in 1951. Within a decade it was explored and charted by the US Navy submersible Trieste.

Across much of the Pacific sea bed are eroded and extinct volcanoes called guyots or tablemounts, many of them hundreds of millions of years old. These are isolated, steep sided and flat topped and are found almost exclusively in the Pacific. A typical guyot lies more than 200 m (656 ft) below the water's surface and can be as much as 10 km (6 miles) in diameter and at least 900 m (2,953 ft) tall. Once they might have protruded above the water line but weather, wind and waves have taken their toll and reduced the overall guyot size.

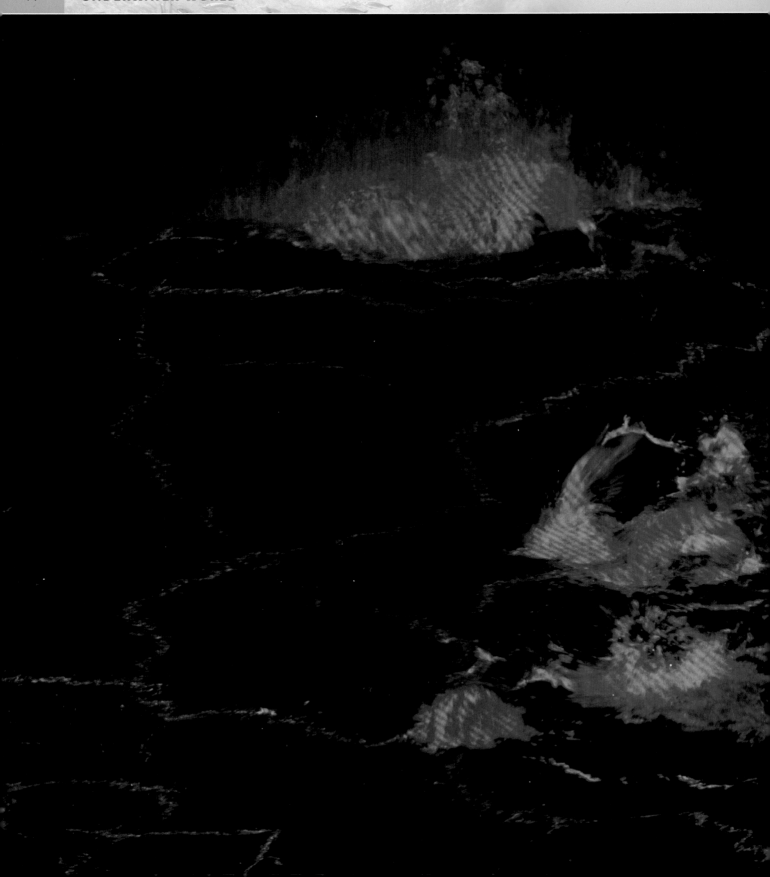

An associated feature is the oceanic plateau or seamount chain. These are huge volcanic constructions made by lava venting through the sea floor millions of years ago. To geologists they demonstrate ancient tectonic plate activity. There are an estimated 2,000 seamounts on the Pacific Ocean bed. One of the biggest formations is the Louisville Seamount Chain over 70 seamounts in the south western Pacific that was only discovered in 1972. Originally formed by hotspot volcano activity it stretches from the Pacific–Antarctic Ridge for 4,300 km (2,672 miles) north west to south east diagonally across the ocean floor to the Tonga-Kermadec Trench where it subducts under the Indo-Australia Plate. The Hawaiian islands are the uneven crown of another seamount chain that includes atolls (islands of coral that encircle lagoons), 80 submarine volcanoes as well as numerous reefs and shallows.

Climate and currents

Thanks to its size, water temperatures in the Pacific vary from freezing in the north to as much as 30°C (86°F) at the equator. Both heavy rainfall at the equator and ice at the poles reduce the salinity in those areas. The main deep water movement is generally a northward progression of cold water from the Antarctic towards the shores of Japan and eastwards towards China.

The winds across the Pacific are in two main belts. There are westerlies which blow from west to east between latitudes 30° and 60°, both north and south of the equator. Meanwhile around the equator there are the trade winds. As the winds blow uninterrupted over such a huge distance there are mighty waves around islands like Hawaii. In late summer and early autumn particularly, the Pacific Ocean is ruffled by the typhoon season.

The surface waters of the Pacific generally move in two huge gyres; the clockwise North Pacific Gyre and the South Pacific Gyre, which runs in reverse. These contribute to and influence other currents to either cool or warm the waters. One particularly unattractive feature of the North Pacific Gyre, with its four contributory currents, is the amount of man-made waste spiralling in its clutches. So great is the amount of plastic debris moving on the water it is known as the Great Pacific garbage patch.

◄ *A lava lake in the Hawaiian Volcanoes National Park; although it is more than 200 years since the last eruption, there is plenty of volcanic activity on the islands.*

EL NINO

At irregular intervals of between two and nine years, El Nino – meaning boy child or Christ child in Spanish – makes it presence felt. Its proper name is El Nino-Southern Oscillation but it is more easily recognised as ENSO.

Its characteristic pressure increase over the Indian Ocean, Indonesia and Australia saps the strength of the trade winds and allows the surface waters around the equator to warm, as explained in the section on 'Effects of winds over the oceans' above.

On the ground, it means Indonesia and India are likely to suffer droughts, Australia will crackle with bush fires thanks to reduced rainfall and suffer poor air quality while the coastal regions of Peru and Ecuador will languish in a washed out summer, accompanied by flooding. The snow in North America is reduced while Europe suffers a warm, wet winter.

Weather conditions like this fall into the El Nino class when the nutrient-poor warm water of the equatorial current overwhelms the cold, fruitful water of the Humboldt current for longer than five months. Its subsequent effect can, however, be long-lived.

▼ *The cyclical El Nino often results in rough coastal surf as demonstrated off the Central California Coast.*

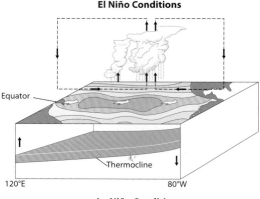

El Niño Conditions

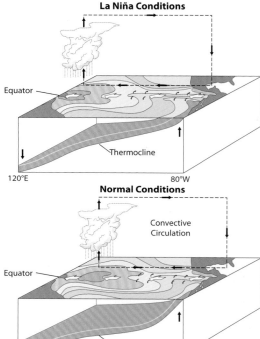

La Niña Conditions

Normal Conditions

▲ *These three diagrams show the difference between normal, El Nino and La Nina conditions.*

The Southern Oscillation component of this formula refers to an atmospheric condition in which the air pressure fluctuates between the tropical eastern and western Pacific.

When surface waters in the eastern Pacific are cooler than normal, the situation is reversed. Known as La Nina, a pool of cold water collects in the eastern Pacific boosting trade winds and increasing rainfall over the American Midwest. Canada will expect a cooler, snowier winter than normal and there will be heavy rain over Indonesia, Malaysia and the Philippines. La Nina – Spanish for the girl – is thought to be critical in reducing global warming by depressing sea surface temperatures.

SEA OF CORTEZ

Although its dimensions are modest – covering a mere 160,000 square kilometers (62,000 square miles) – the Sea of Cortez is one of the most abundant marine environments in the world. So rich is its vein of wildlife that it was branded 'the world's aquarium' by famous French diver Jacques Cousteau.

Also known as the Gulf of California or the Vermillion Sea, its waters are home to over 5,000 species, including manta rays, humpback whales, the blue whale and leatherback turtles. Consequently it has become a honeypot for wildlife watchers. The waters are conducive to a profusion of life thanks to ocean vents that lie in shallow waters, belching out warmth and mineral wealth upon which bacteria flourish to become the root of the area's food chain. All this happens once again because of lively tectonic plate movement.

This comparatively narrow waterway, separating the isolated Baja Peninsula in California from the Mexican mainland, is the meeting point of the North American and Pacific Plates, which are drifting away from each other at a rate of about 2.5 cm (nearly 1 in) a year. Indeed, its northern boundary is better known as the San Andreas Fault, the terrestrial fracture that caused the 1906 San Francisco earthquake in which 3,000 people died.

Also in the Pacific Ocean bracket are the Bering Sea, the Bering Strait, the Gulf of Alaska, the Sea of Japan, the East and South China Seas and the Tasman, Coral, Balie and Java Seas, among others.

▼ *A large pod of long-beaked common dolphin porpoising in the Sea of Cortez.*

ATLANTIC OCEAN

The Atlantic Ocean separates the great continents of Europe and the Americas and, north to south, the Arctic Ocean and the Southern Ocean. Much smaller than the Pacific, the Atlantic Ocean covers about 77 million square kilometers (nearly 30 million square miles).

Unseen by human eyes, ocean creep is increasing the size of the Atlantic at the expense of the Pacific to the tune of about 0.5 square kilometers (0.2 square miles) a year.

The Atlantic Ocean bed

Beneath the waters of the Atlantic lies the longest mountain chain on earth. The Mid-Atlantic Ridge covers almost a third of the Atlantic basin and dates back 180 million years when it ruptured to divide the continents of Europe, Africa and the Americas. It is no less than 10,000 km (6,214 miles) long running from near the North Pole to the sub-Antarctic Bouvet Island. In places this geological wonder is 966 km (600 miles) wide.

Barring a cataclysmic disaster, none of us will ever see the majority of the majestic peaks that form the Mid-Atlantic Ridge. Most of it is about 2,500 m (8,200 ft) below sea level. However, there are a few scraps of evidence that break the waves, including Iceland, the Azores, St Helena, Bermuda, Tristan da Cunha and Ascension Island.

▲ Saunders Island, part of the South Sandwich Islands in the southern Atlantic Ocean, boasts an active stratovolcano in Mount Michael.

▶ The Mid-Atlantic Ridge is the dominating feature of this ocean.

The Atlantic Ocean has few guyots but among them is one of the world's biggest, in the shape of the Great Meteor Tablemount in the north east Atlantic, which stands 4,000 m (13,120 ft) tall and has a diameter of 110 km (68 miles). There are, however, fewer active or dormant volcanoes in the Atlantic than in any other of the world's oceans.

It is also light on deep ocean trenches, with just two to its name. The Puerto Rico Trench is the deepest part of the Atlantic, plunging to 8,648 m (28,373 ft) and, unusually, is located at a boundary between two sliding tectonic plates – the North American and the Caribbean – with consequently very little subduction. The Caribbean Plate slides eastwards at about 2 cm (0.79 in) a year, occasionally sparking earthquakes, submarine landslides, volcanic eruptions and tsunamis.

The South Sandwich Trench runs for 965 km (600 miles) east from the volcanic arc of the South Sandwich Islands. It is the result of subduction between the major South American Plate and its more insignificant cousin, the South Sandwich Plate, and lies only slightly shallower than the Puerto Rico Trench.

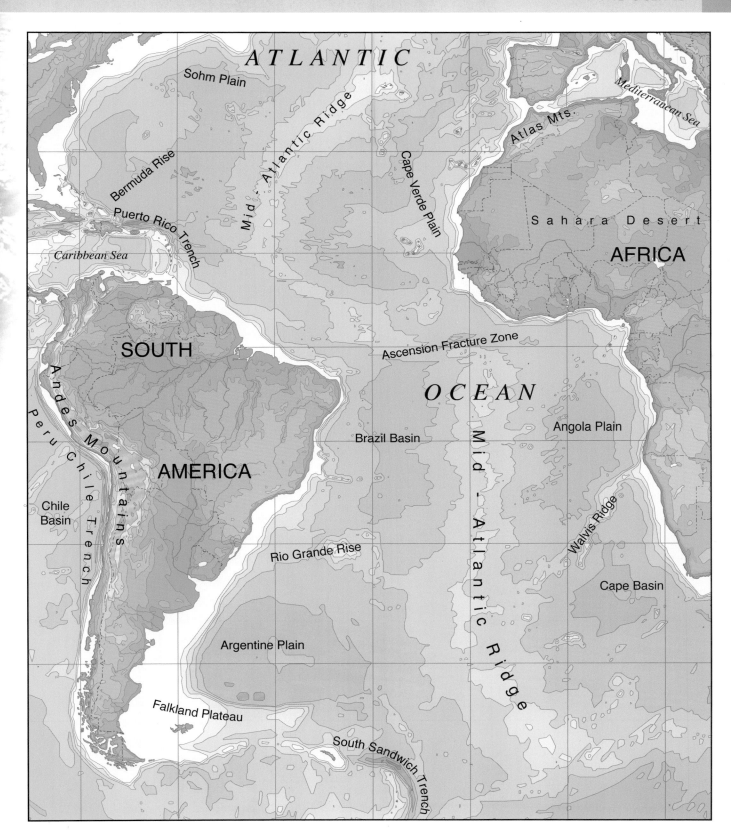

ATLANTIC

Sohm Plain

Mediterranean Sea

Bermuda Rise

Mid - Atlantic Ridge

Atlas Mts.

Cape Verde Plain

Puerto Rico Trench

Sahara Desert

Caribbean Sea

AFRICA

SOUTH

Ascension Fracture Zone

OCEAN

Andes Mountains

AMERICA

Angola Plain

Brazil Basin

Peru Chile Trench

Mid - Atlantic Ridge

Chile
Basin

Walvis Ridge

Rio Grande Rise

Cape Basin

Argentine Plain

Falkland Plateau

South Sandwich Trench

Climate and currents

Atlantic weather varies according to latitude. Westerly winds rush through the higher latitudes, bringing with them changing weather patterns and frequent storms. Meanwhile one of the main features of the lower latitudes in the North Atlantic is the hurricane season of late summer and early autumn. These mighty storms brew in the mid and eastern Atlantic and track north and west to the Caribbean and the North American coast. The warm waters flowing through the Caribbean as well as those off north and east Florida and the greater Antilles are a big draw for hurricanes.

Warm tropical waters meeting colder currents in the central latitudes off the east coast of the US inspire cyclonic storms. Around the equator there are belts of high pressure systems and constant easterly trade winds.

The surface waters of the Atlantic are moved by two large gyres, clockwise in the northern hemisphere and counterclockwise in the southern hemisphere. The North Atlantic Gyre has four distinct currents: the Gulf Stream running from west to east, the North Atlantic Current to the north, the Canary Current on the eastern perimeter running southwards and the North Equatorial Current returning the water westwards.

Of those, perhaps the Gulf Stream is most significant. It circulates from the Caribbean eastwards across the mid-Atlantic to northern Europe. It carries warm salty water to the North Atlantic where it becomes the North Atlantic Drift. Here it cools and sinks to the lower realms of the Norwegian Sea. In winter the warm waters of the Gulf Stream transfer heat into the frigid air masses created over icy Canada, Greenland and Iceland. These air masses move eastwards and make northern Europe much warmer in the winter than comparable latitudes in North America, for example. Put simply, without the Gulf Stream, northern Europe would freeze.

The South Atlantic Gyre is bordered at its southern perimeter by the icy Arctic Circumpolar Current while the eastern edge is formed by the cold Benguela current that flows north up the coast of west Africa. To the west the Brazil current flows from the equator down the east coast of South America.

The Grand Banks are 280,000 square kilometers (about 108,000 square miles) of continental shelf to the east of Newfoundland. Here warm, moist, southerly air condenses as it meets the cold Labrador Current, causing the area's notoriously dense sea fogs.

▼ *Hurricanes and cyclones can soon transform the Atlantic Ocean from idyllic conditions to a malevolent maelstrom.*

◄ *Sargassum weed grows on the sea bottom but will break off to form large floating rafts.*

THE SARGASSO SEA

Far out in the Atlantic lies a sea without a shoreline. There are no cliffs at its edge nor is there frothy surf or wave breaks. Yet the Sargasso Sea has such distinctive characteristics it can be defined amid the water mass of the Atlantic.

It lies at the heart of the North Atlantic Gyre, south east of Bermuda in an area known as both the Horse latitudes – because it is said Spanish sailors trapped in its doldrums threw their horses overboard to conserve fresh water supplies – and the Bermuda Triangle.

In essence it is a large, oval zone of calm, nutrient-poor waters circulating clockwise over an area measuring 1,100 km by 3,200 km (approximately 700 miles by 2,000 miles). It is hedged in by three currents; the Canary in the east, the North Equatorial in the south and the Gulf Stream in the west. The Sargasso Sea is known for its clear, deep blue waters that offer exceptional clarity. There is still visibility in the water even at depths of 61 m (200 ft).

Its waters whipped by the Coriolis effect rise about one meter (3 ft) higher than that of the sea level on the eastern seaboard of the US. In the summer the waters evaporate in the heat, which creates a warm, saline-rich layer across its center. This inhibits the upwelling of nutrient-rich cold water from the ocean depths, making it an unpalatable area for plankton and thus stunting the food chain before it has a chance to begin. What it lacks in marine life, though, it makes up for in seaweed. The Sargasso Sea is noted for its massive mats of yellow-brown sargassum seaweed that smother the ocean's surface. It floats thanks to small, grape-like air sacs. Indeed, early Portuguese explorers named the area for sargaço, meaning grape. And thanks to the seaweed there are some marine creatures at home here, namely small octopuses, shrimp, sea worms and small crabs; and it is the ideal environment for the cleverly camouflaged sargassum fish, which is indistinguishable from the seaweed.

More curiously still, all the river-dwelling eels of the eastern US and Europe are born in the Sargasso Sea. Between the ages of 10 and 15 years, eels migrate there to mate and lay eggs. Once the elvers hatch, they are carried back thousands of kilometers by the Gulf Stream to their home rivers in North America and Europe.

Given the rolling action of the currents, it is hardly surprising to find that the Sargasso Sea is also a notorious repository for rubbish.

Other waterways that form part of the Atlantic include the Hudson Bay, the Gulf of St Lawrence, the Gulf of Mexico, the Caribbean Sea, the Denmark Straight, the Norwegian and North Seas, the Bay of Biscay, the Black and Baltic Seas and the Strait of Magellan.

▼ *This clump of Sargassum weed provides these Atlantic spotted dolphins with something to play with.*

INDIAN OCEAN

Sitting between the Indian subcontinent, the east coast of Africa, Australasia and the Southern Ocean are the predominantly warm and tropical waters of the Indian Ocean.

Although it is less than half the size of the Pacific it still musters a generous 10,000 km (6,214 miles) of width between the east coast of Africa and the west coast of Australia. And the Indian Ocean contains a fifth of all the world's waters because it runs pretty deep. The deepest points lie in the Sunda Trench – also known as the Java Trench – some 7,725 m (25,344 ft) deep and the Diamantina Trench, south west of Perth, Australia, which is 300 m (984 ft) deeper still.

It was formed at the same time as the Southern Ocean some 120 million years ago, making it one of the youngest oceans. Its mid-ocean ridges are also still active. The sheer volume of oceanic crust that the ridges produce is gradually pushing Australia, Africa and Antarctica away from each other and very slowly increasing the size of the Indian Ocean itself.

Indian Ocean bed

As well as the deposits spewed forth by the Indian Ocean's ridge system that spreads its colossal limbs across the sea floor, there are huge deposits of silt carried along the vast submarine canyons cut into it by the weighty outflows of immense rivers like the Ganges, the Indus and the Zambezi.

At its north east leading edge the Indian Plate is being overwhelmed by the Eurasian Plate, which has created the still-active volcanic arcs of Sumatra and Java.

The Indian Ocean is characterized by clusters of coral islands, numbering in the thousands. These include the Seychelles, the Maldives and countless others with uniformly azure seas lapping against pristine coral reefs. There are some 4,000 species of fish living in the Indian Ocean, thriving in the warm, clear waters and providing a square meal for predators and fishermen alike.

But there's trouble in paradise from two primary sources. The first is the potential of climate change to increase the level of the sea so considerably that many of these idyllic isles will be swamped. The second is the threat of underwater earthquakes and ensuing tsunamis. More of this later.

Climate and currents

Seasonal monsoons are a hallmark of the climate in the north Indian Ocean, brought in on rain-bearing winds that switch direction twice a year. Strong north east winds blow from October to May. However, between May and October the winds blow from the south and west. This is accompanied by a bi-yearly change in direction of the primary current, a phenomenon unique to the Indian Ocean. In the southern hemisphere the winds are generally gentler but can whip up sudden and severe summer storms.

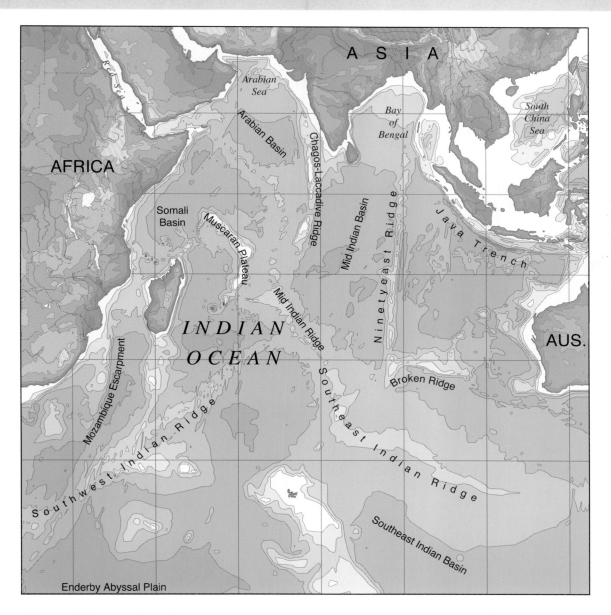

The map of the Indian Ocean with labels:

A S I A

Red Sea

Arabian Sea

Arabian Basin

Bay of Bengal

South China Sea

AFRICA

Chagos-Laccadive Ridge

Somali Basin

Muscaran Plateau

Mid Indian Basin

Ninetyeast Ridge

Java Trench

INDIAN OCEAN

Mid Indian Ridge

AUS.

Mozambique Escarpment

Southwest Indian Ridge

Southeast Indian Ridge

Broken Ridge

Southeast Indian Basin

Enderby Abyssal Plain

◀ *Ari Atoll, one of 26 islands that make up the Republic of Maldives in the Indian Ocean.*

▲ *The Indian Ocean accounts for around 20 per cent of the water on the Earth's surface.*

Monsoons start as tropical storms gathering over the open ocean before heading westwards. The north east monsoon season, or winter monsoon, lasts from December to April while the south west monsoon season is from June to October. The heavy rains are welcome as a break from the long, hot, arid weather that burns much of continental east and southern Africa, southern India and Australasia, and are vital for the survival of wildlife, people and crops.

Another typical Indian Ocean weather pattern is the tropical cyclone that originates in the doldrums near the equator and then blows over the northern Indian Ocean in May and June,

and again in October and November and across the southern Indian Ocean in January and February.

The Indian Ocean has four principal currents: the North Equatorial Current, the Mozambique – or South Equatorial – current, the Agulhas Stream and the West Wind Drift Current. Southern Indian Ocean waters are given direction by the counterclockwise South Indian Gyre that drives the Mozambique current. This flows southwards from the equator down the East African coast to about 35°S where it becomes the warm Agulhas Stream.

TSUNAMI

Tsunamis can occur anywhere in the world. In fact, they are most frequently found in the Pacific. But when a tsunami is generated in the Indian Ocean, more countries and their populations are in peril, largely due to the curvature of the land around it.

The tectonic plate upon which India squats has been slowly moving north east for millions of years and as a consequence the Himalayas have erupted. The process continues and it can produce some earth-shakers. Other seismically intense areas include the Makran coast of Pakistan and the shore regions of Maharashtra in India. Most tsunamis in the Indian Ocean are started by large earthquakes in the still-active subduction zones around the Indian Ocean.

It was just such an event that caused the 2004 Indian Ocean tsunami that killed 230,000 people in 14 countries after islands and resorts were inundated with water. The earthquake, measuring at least 9 on the Richter Scale, was perhaps the second largest in history. It occurred 30 km (19 miles) underwater 240 km (150 miles) off the coast of Sumatra and shook the ground in Indonesia for eight minutes. But worse was to follow. The shift of some 20 m (66 ft) in the ocean floor dispatched a series of waves that built up awesome velocity as they approached the shore. They first hit Sumatra 30 minutes after the earth stopped trembling. There was little or no warning and devastation was widespread.

▲ *A fishing trawler, swept inland onto Alaska's Kenai Peninsula, demonstrates the power of a tsunami.*

Before 2004 the most notorious tsunami known occurred following the Krakatoa eruption; this island volcano in the Sundra Strait between Java and Sumatra had been silent for some 200 years before literally blowing its top on August 26, 1883. Many thousands of people died, not principally from the volcanic eruption but from the devastating tsunamis that followed.

Also incorporated into the Indian Ocean is the Andaman Sea, the Bay of Bengal, the Red Sea, the Persian Gulf, the Arabian Sea, the Great Australian Bight, the Java Sea and the Strait of Malacca.

▶ *A magnitude 9.0 earthquake - the largest in 40 years - struck offshore of the Indonesian island of Sumatra on December 26, 2004.*

ARCTIC OCEAN

The seas that surround the north polar ice cap cover about 14 million square kilometers (5.4 million square miles) and touch the shores of North America, Russia and Europe. Nonetheless, the Arctic Ocean remains the smallest in the world.

Most of the Arctic Ocean waters come from the Atlantic while there is seepage from the Pacific through the narrow and shallow Bering Strait. In addition, huge volumes of fresh water gush into it from great rivers including Canada's Mackenzie River and the River Ob in Siberia.

Although it looks like one body of water, the Arctic has two distinct characteristics. The Arctic basin is a central depression averaging 4000 m (13,123 ft) in depth. It is hemmed in by a continental shelf, slashing the depth, upon which archipelagos and islands are perched.

Think of the Arctic and a picture of endless ice comes to mind. In fact, about a third of the Arctic Ocean is permanently covered with pack ice at latitudes above 75°N. The rest, lying between 60°

and 75°N, is covered with sea ice in winter, at which time the ice cap almost doubles in size. Against expectation, the Arctic waters are generally warmer than the air temperature.

As the Arctic hugs the northern axis of the earth its waters lie in continual darkness between November and February and glisten in round-the-clock daylight between May and August.

▶ *NASA and the National Snow and Ice Data Center studies confirm that sea ice cover is continuing to shrink in tandem with the ice cap thinning.*

▶ The Arctic Circle is an imaginary line located at 66°, 30'N latitude, and defines the southernmost part of the Arctic.

PACIFIC OCEAN

Hawaiian Ridge

Northwest Pacific Basin

Mariana Trench

Japan Trench

Aleutian Trench

Kuril - Kamchatka Trench

JAPAN

Bering Sea

Aleutian Basin

Sea of Japan

NORTH KOREA

SOUTH KOREA

East China Sea

Sea of Okhotsk

Yellow Sea

PHILIPPINES

South China Sea

Gulf of Alaska

Arctic Circle

Chukchi Sea

Rocky Mountains

NORTH

CANADA

Beaufort Sea

Canada Basin

Leptev Sea

Gobi Desert

MONGOLIA

AMERICA

ARCTIC OCEAN

+ North Pole

ASIA

MYANMAR

CHINA

BHUTAN

U.S.A.

RUSSIA

Plateau of Tibet

NEPAL

Hudson Bay

Kara Sea

KYRGYZSTAN

INDIA

Baffin Island

Baffin Bay

KAZAKHSTAN

TAJIKISTAN

Greenland Sea

UZBEKISTAN

AFGHANISTAN

PAKISTAN

GREENLAND

Barents Sea

Aral Sea

Labrador Basin

TURKMENISTAN

Norwegian Sea

ICELAND

FINLAND

Caspian Sea

IRAN

Charlie - Gibbs Fracture Zone

NORWAY SWEDEN

ESTONIA

Baltic Sea

LITHUANIA

LATVIA

BELARUS

EUROPE

Caucasus

North Sea

DENMARK

POLAND

UKRAINE

MOLDOVA

Black Sea

TURKEY

IRAQ

ATLANTIC OCEAN

Mid - Atlantic Ridge

IRELAND

U.K.

NETH.

GERMANY

CZECH

SLOVAKIA

ROMANIA

SYRIA

LEBANON

SAUDI ARABIA

BELGIUM

LUX.

SWITZERLAND

AUSTRIA

HUNGARY

SLOVENIA CROATIA

BOSNIA & HERZ.

SERBIA & MONT.

BULGARIA

ISRAEL JORDAN

FRANCE

Alps

ITALY

ALBANIA

MACEDONIA

GREECE

Red Sea

ANDORRA

PORTUGAL

SPAIN

TUNISIA

Mediterranean Sea

EGYPT

Atlas Mts.

WESTERN SAHARA

MOROCCO

Canary Islands

ALGERIA

LIBYA

SUDAN

MAURITANIA

MALI

NIGER

CHAD

Sahara Desert

Ice

The ice that is abundant in the Arctic and the Southern Ocean is crucial for stabilizing the Earth's climate as it insulates large areas of water from solar radiation in the summer while additionally preventing heat loss in the winter.

Ecologists and climate watchers are concerned that the polar ice cap is slowly eroding thanks to climate change. This would not, in itself, impact global sea levels that much because the ice is already floating, but it will restrict the cover the ice provides in the ocean by reflecting back solar rays. If the ice melts, more solar rays will be absorbed in the Arctic Ocean, which will subsequently get warmer and speed the melting process.

Icebergs – taken from the Dutch for ice mountain – litter the Arctic, North Atlantic and the Southern Ocean and are a perpetual danger to shipping. Buoyant icebergs are made of

fresh water rather than sea water as they are created when ice sheers away from glaciers, other, larger icebergs or from the ice shelf. Essentially they were once snow that fell to earth years before. An iceberg can come in all shapes and sizes, from an ice chunk to an ice island.

An iceberg looks large and overarching from the surface of the water. Nonetheless that is only a fraction of its true height and girth as almost nine tenths of it will be lying treacherously out of sight, beneath the waves. This is because the average density of an iceberg is about 87 per cent that of seawater.

After the loss of the Titanic in 1912 an International Ice Patrol was established to monitor the progress of dangerous icebergs free-ranging in the shipping lanes and warn ships of their existence. Today the patrol uses planes, radar and even satellite

data to ensure the peril posed by icebergs is mitigated.

One of the main sources of icebergs in the North Atlantic is the glacier region of western Greenland; the glaciers here are fast moving and cover up to 7 km (4.3 miles). Drifting south in the Labrador Current they head for Iceberg Alley, which extends south along the coast of Newfoundland. It takes about three years for enormous icebergs to reach Newfoundland, however, as they must cover a distance of 1,600 nautical miles (nearly 3000 km).

The largest northern hemisphere iceberg on record was spotted near Baffin Island in 1882. It was 13 km (8 miles) long, 6 km (4 miles) wide and its height above water was about 20 m (66 ft). The mass of that single iceberg was more than 9 billion tonnes (9.9 billion US tons)– enough water for everyone in the world to drink one liter a day for over four years. Meanwhile, the tallest iceberg spotted in the North Atlantic was 168 m (551 ft) high.

Strong winds and currents keep the pack ice in constant motion in the Arctic, sometimes opening up cracks and pools. However, as the Arctic Ocean is largely encircled by land, the movement of the sea ice is restricted. As the ice moves it breaks into ragged pieces that then pile up creating ice ridges up to 5 m (16 ft) high, a distinctive feature of Arctic ice.

▼ *The Arctic Ocean is a particular area of concern for those who believe in climate change. Here surface melt water adorns the solid pack ice.*

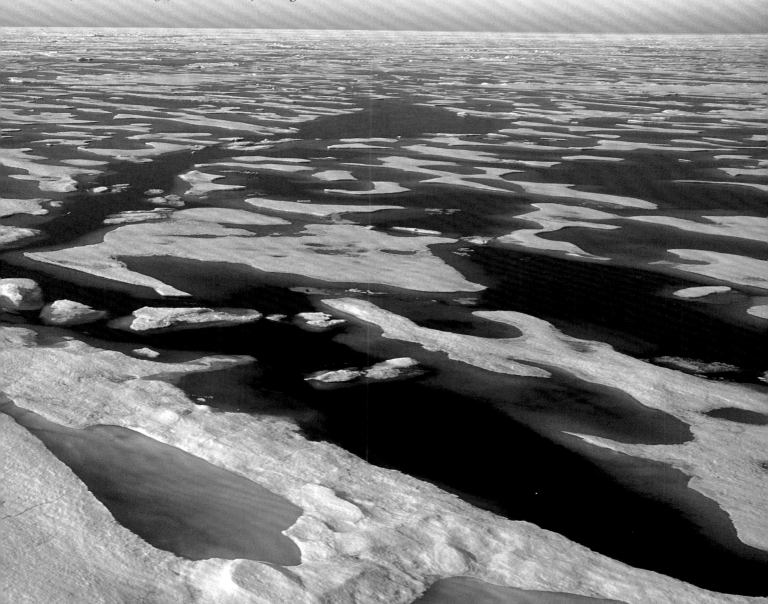

◄ *Despite the harsh environment, numerous species – such as the polar bear – have adapted to survive in the Arctic.*

Climate and currents

Two principal currents stir the waters of the Arctic; the east to west Transpolar Drift from the Chuckchi Sea to the Greenland Sea north of Siberia and the clockwise Beaufort Gyre that rotates across the Beaufort Sea and around the North Pole, north of Canada and Alaska.

The Beaufort Gyre is driven by high pressure system winds blowing in a clockwise circulation around the Pole. This gyre is so powerful that it rotates the entire polar ice cap through a 360 degree turn about every four years. From time to time, usually after a low-pressure system passes across the area, the Beaufort Gyre will completely reverse its direction for a few days.

So thanks to the quirks of this robust Beaufort Gyre, sea ice caught in its grip can become trapped and circulate around the Arctic for several years, growing thicker and more compacted and ridged than elsewhere.

The Transpolar Drift sends cold water and sea ice westwards from Siberia, across the Arctic basin then into the North Atlantic towards the east and north coast of Greenland and Canada. Like the Beaufort Gyre, it will occasionally reverse direction for a short time. Its thrust helps to compress ice against land, helping to create the thickest ice in the Arctic.

The Arctic Ocean encompasses Baffin Bay, the Beaufort Sea, the Barents Sea, the Chuckchi Sea, the Greenland Sea and the White Sea.

▶ *A panoramic view of icebergs at midnight in Disko Bay near Ilulissat, western Greenland.*

SOUTHERN OCEAN

The newest of the world's oceans – designated in 2000 by the scientists of the International Hydrographic Organization – the Southern Ocean laps Antarctica. But what it lacks in age, it makes up for in menace. Across the Southern Ocean the strongest average wind speeds on the planet blow, helping to create the most hostile seas in the world.

It shares a demarcation line with the Antarctic Treaty, first signed in 1961 and intended to save the icy wastes of Antarctica – the only continent without a native population – for scientific research. As a consequence, all military activity is banned.

Much of the Southern Ocean's 20 million square kilometers (7.8 million square miles) is covered with ice for the majority of the year. At its densest, the 2.5 km (1.6 mile) deep ice cap covering Antarctica is so heavy that it actually depresses the land, which in turn pushes the surrounding continental shelf much deeper than elsewhere on Earth.

At its coldest, the pack ice in Antarctica grows up to eight times larger than in summer, from an average minimum of 2.6 million square kilometers (1 million square miles) to around 18.8 million square kilometers (7.26 million square miles).

▼ *A humpback whale surfaces near an iceberg at Prospect Point, Antarctica.*

▶ *The Earth's newest ocean, the Southern Ocean is generally taken to be south of 60°S latitude and encircles Antarctica.*

AUSTRALIA

AUSTRALIA

Tasman Sea

NEW CALEDONIA

FIJI

Tonga Trench

Kermadic Trench

Chattenger Plateau

PACIFIC

NEW ZEALAND
Chateau Rise

Southwest Pacific Basin

Campbell Plateau

OCEAN

Great Australian Bight
S. Australia Basin

Southeast Indian Ridge

Eltanin Fracture Zone

Pacific - Antarctic Ridge

Udintsev Fracture Zone

East Pacific Rise

SOUTHERN OCEAN

INDIAN

Australian - Antarctic Basin

Southeast Indian Ridge

South Indian Basin

Ross Sea

Bellingshausen Plain

Amundsen Sea

Ninety East Ridge

ANTARCTICA

Peru Basin

OCEAN

Kerguelen Plateau

Bellingshausen Sea

Chile Basin

Weddell Sea

Peru Chile Trench

Andes Mountains

CHILE

PERU

SOUTHERN OCEAN

Enderby Abyssal Plain

Weddel Abyssal Plain

America-Antarctic Ridge

South Georgia Rise

FALKLAND ISLANDS

ARGENTINA

BOLIVIA

Southwest Indian Ridge

SOUTH GEORGIA ISLAND

Falkland Plain

URUGUAY

PARAGUAY

MADAGASCAR

Argentine Basin

BRAZIL

MOZAMBIQUE

SWAZILAND LESOTHO

ZIMBABWE

SOUTH AFRICA

BOTSWANA

Mid Atlantic Ridge

ATLANTIC

Cape Basin

OCEAN

Brazil Basin

ZAMBIA

NAMIBIA

ANGOLA

Angola Basin

The ice cycle

Sea ice forms in layers. The first stage is grease ice, when the sea water starts to form loose but thick masses of slippery ice crystals. As these slowly harden and thicken up, wave action breaks the surface into separate pieces turning the ice to platelets. In turn the platelets collide with each other and, as the edges curl up under the impact, they form oval shapes fittingly called pancake ice. This ice slowly thickens until, after about 12 months, it is around 30 cm (12 in) thick, when it is known as first year ice. Over the summer months this partially melts and then builds up again through winter. Over a period of years the ice can become up to 10 m (33 ft) thick, by which time it is known as multiyear ice.

Fast ice is sea ice that is anchored by the land or the ocean floor. It freezes into a slushy crust around the shore and, once hardened, it remains attached to the coast for the season. Consequently it doesn't move with the wind and waves and can even act as a trap for passing drift ice – newly frozen sea ice. The two can fuse together although they have radically different depths. Accordingly the heavier drift ice brings unbearable tension to bear on the fast ice and the result is a pattern of fractures.

Even sturdy fast ice is subject to the whim of the sea, which swells and recedes with each tide. This action creates a feature known as tide cracks, which open up with the high tide and close again as it ebbs. Tide cracks are never very wide but can be many kilometers long and are a valuable lifeline for oxygen-breathing animals including seals, and are hunting grounds for fisher birds like snow petrels.

From fast ice there comes pack ice. Pack ice is defined as sea water that has been frozen elsewhere for a minimum of a year, broken up by the melt and has then drifted in the clutches of the winds and the currents before re-freezing the following winter. It makes for heavy ice and accumulations of 100 m (328 ft) or more have a calming effect on the ocean swell. As it takes less time for still water to freeze than for moving water, the pack ice speeds the icing up process. Ice floes are small, floating ice fragments that split from pack ice.

After building up over winter the Antarctic ice pack melts in the face of warmer weather and vast icebergs are liberated from the ice shelf in a process known as calving and drift into the wider waters of the Southern Ocean. Smallish icebergs – about the size of a car – are known as growlers thanks to the noise they make. Difficult to spot in the water, these are particularly hazardous to ships. The Antarctic is populated with tabular icebergs, with flat tops and steep sides which at least are easy to see coming. Ice formed from a small section of a much larger iceberg left floating in the water is known as a bergy bit.

The largest icebergs – perhaps more accurately called ice islands – originate from the vast ice shelves surrounding Antarctica, which is where 93 per cent of world's icebergs are found. Antarctic ice shelves may calve icebergs that are over 80 km (50 miles) long.

Around the edges of the Antarctic are the enormous Ross Ice Shelf and the Ronne-Filchner Ice Shelf. Originating from snow, they contain fresh water, as of course do the icebergs they calve.

▼ *The waters of the Southern Ocean carve some magnificent structures in the ice.*

In 1987, an iceberg with an area of 6,350 square kilometers (2,452 square miles) broke from the Ross Ice Shelf in Antarctica. It held within its icy grasp a mass of around 1.4 trillion tonnes and could have supplied everyone in the world with 240 tonnes of pure drinking water.

The ice shelves are distinguished by high cliffs at their seaward edge, as much as 60 m (197 ft) above water. They are likely to extend a further 900 meters (3,000 ft) below the water line. These substantial shelves act like a brake and prevent vast quantities of Antarctic ice from reaching the Southern Ocean. If Antarctic ice were let loose and melted in large amounts, it would lead to a global catastrophe for low lying areas. One estimate reckons that, if Antarctica were to melt, the sea level would rise by a mighty 60 m (197 ft).

▲ *The Ross Ice Shelf was named after Sir James Clark Ross, commander of a British Admiralty expedition to determine the true position of the South Magnetic Pole in 1841.*

Seawater circulates underneath part of the ice shelf, where some of it slowly solidifies rejecting the saline content as it freezes. The remaining sea water gets colder, denser and more saline and sinks down to the continental shelf where it glides along the sea floor away from the Pole into deeper waters. Much of the cold, dense water on the ocean beds of the world originally formed beneath the Ronne-Filchner Ice Shelf.

Climate and currents

Waters in the Antarctic generally move in a clockwise direction with smaller rotations in the Weddell Sea and the Ross Sea, although there are a number of currents that drive local conditions. However, in general terms, sea ice gradually moves away from the Pole into warmer waters, where it melts.

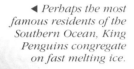

◀ Perhaps the most famous residents of the Southern Ocean, King Penguins congregate on fast melting ice.

The largest ocean current on earth is the Antarctic Circumpolar Current (ACC), also known as the West Wind Drift, that slowly flows eastwards around the Antarctic driven by westerly winds and unhindered by land masses. However, the ocean bed with its troughs and ridges – including the Pacific–Antarctic Ridge and Drake Passage – directs the flow and contributes a level of drag which slows the speed of the deeper water.

The ACC extends from the surface to depths of up to 4,000 m (13,123 ft) and can be as wide as 2,000 km (1,243 miles). In the process it transports more water than any other system on earth. The current links the three great basins of the Pacific, Atlantic and Indian Oceans, swapping water, chemicals – particularly salts – animals and warmth between them.

In addition, the ACC acts as a barrier against the warmer ocean waters reaching Antarctica and protects the ice cap. This deep water current is thought to affect the climate in several ways. The annual freeze and thaw helps to create the upwellings in the Southern Ocean and so the waters of the southerly zones are continually renewed and reinvigorated. The current helps to redistribute heat and nutrients and it has a significant effect on climate by influencing rainfall and temperature across the southern waters.

Moreover the ocean can sink 50 times more carbon than the atmosphere. Its surface exchanges gases like oxygen and carbon dioxide and this function directly affects the climate, particularly around South America, southern Africa and southern Australia.

These deep water currents are created by the changes in density of water masses, usually through the downwelling of dense, cold, heavily saline water like that from beneath the Antarctic ice shelves.

The Atlantic Convergence Zone is the area where cold, saline, Antarctic waters meet the warmer waters that they will sink beneath. This zone surrounds Antarctica between latitudes 50° and 60° S, roughly 200 km (124 miles) off Antarctica. The Circumpolar Deep Water is a zone of continuous upwelling, retrieving deep, nutritious waters from the depths. It occupies the same zone as the ACC. The upwellings provide a rich habitat in which krill feed from plankton and in turn become food for fish, seals, whales and birds.

At their warmest, Southern Ocean waters achieve a high of about 10°C (50°F). Of course underwater, even in winter, the temperature will only descend to the uniform deep water level of 2°C (35.6°F).

The Southern Ocean includes other waters like the Amundsen Sea, the Weddell Sea, the Filchner-Ronne Ice Shelf, the Ross Sea and Ross Ice Shelf and the Bellinghausen Sea.

Animal Life

Marine mammals such as whales, dolphins, seals, manatees and sea otters are nature's crowd pleasers. Though comparatively few in number, their intelligence and often extraordinary antics provide endless fascination for ocean-watchers. In evolutionary terms these animals are the link between the world we inhabit and the mysterious seas we barely know.

▲ *A female humpback whale with her calf.*

ARTHROPODS

▲ The shed moult of a shore crab on saltmarsh on the south coast of England.

Three out of every four animals on the planet are arthropods and they dominate all habitats on earth. Although they are no longer restricted to the sea, it is where they came from and there is fossil evidence to suggest that they moved up the shoreline in not a single, but a series, of invasions.

But when flies, spiders, scorpions and so forth emerged on to dry land – where many later developed wings – they left behind some cousins in the ocean, including crabs, krill, lobsters and, the most abundant of them all, copepods. There are so many copepods in the seas of the world that, although each is tiny, their combined weight is in excess of the total tonnage of whales in the oceans. That astonishing fact points to one inescapable conclusion: Arthropods are the runaway success story of life on Earth.

One contributory factor to the ecological accomplishments of the arthropods is the way their bodies are made. They have a

◄ One member of the arthropod family comes out of a confrontation better than its opponent as a common lobster devours an edible crab.

hard, protective skeleton on the outside rather than the inside of their skin. Called an exoskeleton or carapace, it is primarily made of chitin, a derivative of glucose, protein and calcium. In order that the exoskeleton is a benefit rather than a burden it is jointed to permit efficient movement.

Still, there is one drawback to an exoskeleton that cannot be side-stepped. It does not grow with its owner like skin so it must be shed and replaced. In the short period after the old cover has been discarded and before the new one has hardened the creature depending on it for protection is vulnerable to attack by predators.

In addition, the bigger the exoskeleton the greater the weight the creature beneath must bear. No coincidence then that the creatures with the heaviest load, the crustaceans, have largely stayed in the oceans where the water helps with buoyancy.

Under the exoskeleton the body of an arthropod is divided into segments, many of which have a pair of jointed appendages attached. Of course, some are effectively limbs used for locomotion. Others are more like mouth parts. The appendages might also be used as antennae to sense what's going on in the vicinity or as a way of attracting a mate.

Another key to the success of the arthropods lies in the complexities of their nervous systems which keeps them alert and even leaves them capable of learned behavior, according to some scientific research.

In the ocean there are two major groups of arthropods, the mandibulates and the chelicerates.

One of the *Portunus convexus* species, this red-legged swimming crab traverses the ocean depths.

Mandibulates

Better known as crustaceans, this group includes many creatures, from tiny zooplankton to large lobsters, encompassing crabs, krill and barnacles along the way. The unifying factor is the pair of appendages that extends from the heads of them all, modified for chewing food.

Crustaceans have three main body regions: the head, thorax and abdomen. In some species the head and thorax are fused together in what is called a cephalothorax. Alone among the arthropods they have two antennae of different lengths. They have legs for walking and frequently other legs specially adapted for swimming, called swimmerets. Those with ten legs, which include crabs, lobsters and true shrimp, are called decapods.

Young crustaceans molt frequently and the time between each shell-shedding procedure is short. With age the process slows until they might stop molting entirely. Glands in a crustacean's head secrete specific hormones that inspire the need to molt. One species of krill, *Euphausia superba*, can molt so quickly that, if alarmed, they will literally jump out of their skins. The discarded carapace then acts like a decoy while the krill makes its getaway.

Crabs

A culinary delicacy, crabs (Brachyura) are a sought-after seafood. In fact, of the 5,000 different species of crab, only a few types are suitable for cooking.

A Sally lightfoot crab feeds on a marine iguana hatchling.

Crabs have ten legs and walk sideways, in a pull-push motion, rather than with forward propulsion. Most live out to sea, although there are a few crabs which choose to live on land. Some crabs, but not all, can swim and, to enable them to do so, their last pair of legs has evolved into broad paddles.

With apparently sharp eyes that are out on stalks (but can be lowered for protection) and disproportionately large pincers, or chelas, on the end of two appendages called chelipeds, they are perpetually poised to attack prey. It is thanks to their pincers that they can tackle smaller crabs than themselves, mollusks in shells and small gastropods, although they will also feast on worms, algae and anything they can find bumping along the bottom of the ocean, even mud and sand.

Chelas are important not only for holding food but also for digging and warning off would-be attackers. Helpfully, if a claw breaks off another will grow in its place. The chelas pass food towards the mouth where there are pairs of short appendages to help chew it.

Marine crabs breathe underwater using gills located under their shells. Crabs can also hear well which is important in species where leg-rattling or pincer thudding forms part of the courtship ritual.

The sexes are separate. After the male has delivered the sperm using abdominal appendages called copulatory pleopods the female has the option to store sperm for some time. Eggs leave her body through the chamber containing the sperm and are duly fertilized en route. A female crab tends to clutch the eggs to the hairs on her stomachs until they hatch, when she will wave her body to and fro to assist in the release of the larvae, called zoea. These tiny creatures look nothing like mature crabs and are most remarkable for having huge, compound eyes and spines on their backs which, it is thought, deter predators.

The world's biggest crab is the Japanese spider crab (*Macrocheira kaempferi*), which is to be found on the ocean floor of the north Pacific. With its 3.7 m (12 ft) leg span, its spread is bigger than an average man. On land the largest specimen is the coconut crab (*Birgus latro*), with the comparatively modest leg span of 75 cm (2.5 ft).

Despite their high-level protection, crabs are still prey for other sea creatures, including octopuses, which have a suitably shaped beak-like mouth to crack open the dense shell.

About 500 of all crab species are hermit crabs which, because of their softer carapace, make a home in discarded shells on the ocean floor. For them there's double jeopardy to deal with, when their carapace molts and when their second-hand home becomes too small.

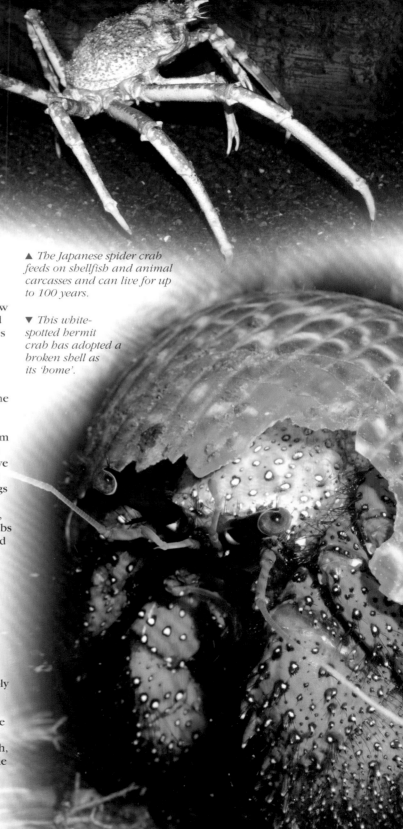

▲ *The Japanese spider crab feeds on shellfish and animal carcasses and can live for up to 100 years.*

▼ *This white-spotted hermit crab has adopted a broken shell as its 'home'.*

Barnacles

Among the most familiar but perhaps least obvious of the crustaceans is the barnacle (Cirripedia). The only sessile crustacean, it is common-place on rocks, shells, coral and the hulls of ships. When they gather in numbers on ships these tiny creatures punch above their weight in terms of pest power, as they slow the vessel down by increasing its drag in the water.

Although they have a preference for shallow waters and intertidal zones, barnacles also latch on to whales and large fish. Immoveable beneath a multi-plated shell of calcium carbonate, the barnacle is inert when its site is exposed by a low tide. Only when covered by water does the shell open to reveal six feathery appendages called cirri, responsible for filtering food from the water. It is these appendages that will beat rhythmically to attract plankton to the shell, counter-balancing the disadvantage of being perpetually stationary. In the absence of gills the cirri are also responsible for absorbing oxygen from the water. Its single eye is probably only capable of detecting whether it is light or dark.

Sometimes the shell is attached directly to a hard surface while other species make use of a stalk. It is fixed in place by cement issued from glands that are usually found at the base of the antennae. They are particularly noticeable when they form a crust in their chosen environment, with numerous barnacles banding together. It is called swamping and it is done so that predators are less likely to annihilate a colony when it comes under attack. Barnacles also aim to grow as large as possible in the shortest time in order to resist competitive species including mussels, limpets and fellow barnacles who want to settle on the same spot. Although they add to the size of their shell with calcified material, barnacles do not molt their plates, although they do shed the cuticle that surrounds it.

Barnacles are hermaphrodites, which means each can fertilize its neighbor, having a comparatively long penis, that can extend through an operculum in the shell, and an egg. Fertilized eggs are brooded within the shell until larvae have developed. One adult barnacle releases about 10,000 nauplius larvae; those that survive will each develop into a cyprid larva, which will attach itself via its antennae to a carefully-selected final resting place and await metamorphosis into adulthood. Although small, both larval forms are nektonic rather than planktonic, that is, they can move independently of currents and tides.

There are about 1,200 known barnacle species. One of the more unusual is the predator barnacle (*Saccula* sp.) which lives under the abdominal plate of crabs, thriving on body tissues. An afflicted crab loses its masculinity and turns into a female. Mussels, whelks and starfish are a barnacle's most common predators.

▶ *Leaf barnacles are often found on rocky shores in the north east Atlantic Ocean.*

◀ *As well as being a common sight in tidal zones, barnacles are also often found on larger marine inhabitants such as this gray whale.*

Lobsters

There are two different kinds of lobster, true and spiny. They are easy to distinguish as true lobsters (Nephropidae, sometimes also called Homaridae) are the only ones to have claws on their first four legs and tend towards cold water, while spiny lobsters (Palinuridae) boast a pair of horns above the eyes and are happiest where the sea is warm. They are not close relatives and it is clawed lobsters that arouse most attention.

A male lobster is known as a cock and a female, a hen. They can be distinguished because the swimmerets in males are hard while in females they are like feathers. The female also has a wide tail to help protect her eggs.

As lobsters grow they molt regularly and will frequently eat their old shell to help rejuvenate the calcium levels of their bodies. It takes between six and eight weeks for a new carapace to harden, during which time they will hide out in sand or seaweed. A lobster aged up to seven years will probably undergo this process about 25 times a year. Later, as fully formed adults, they will do so only once every three or four years. At every molt they can expect to increase their

size by about a fifth. One of the advantages of the molt is that missing appendages can be regenerated; a lobster will sometimes 'amputate' its own appendage in order to escape danger.

It is following molting that female lobsters are most likely to mate, after which they might transport the sperm around with them for up to two years before initiating the fertilization process. Female lobsters then carry eggs the size of a pinhead by the thousand, adhered to their swimmerets. Larvae will molt six times while still in the egg.

There is no further maternal care after the hatched larvae are shaken free by the mother. They float to the ocean's surface for between four to six weeks where they are extremely vulnerable to fish and birds. Only a fraction of one per cent of the eggs released by a lobster will survive into adulthood.

◀ *The American lobster thrives in the cold, shallow waters of the Atlantic where there are many rocks and other places to hide from predators.*

▼ *The European spiny lobster lives on rocky exposed coasts below the tidal zone of the eastern Atlantic Ocean.*

True lobsters eat crabs, mollusks, sea urchins and sea stars. They will only show cannibalistic tendencies if they are trapped in a tank in overcrowded conditions.

Spiny lobsters (Panulirus argus) band together for journeys across the seabed it is thought for protection, and are known to link up one behind another so as to travel in a column. Other lobsters have been seen walking 'hand in hand'.

A lobster that looks pink on a plate is more likely to have been olive green, blue green or even yellowy brown in the sea. The pink pigment only dominates after the cooking process.

Two of the largest lobsters on record were caught off the coast of Virginia in 1934, with one measuring more than a meter (3.3 ft) in length. They weighed 19 kg (42 lbs) and 17 kg (37 lbs).

▶ *Spanish slipper lobsters are not true lobsters, but are more closely related to spiny lobsters and furry lobsters.*

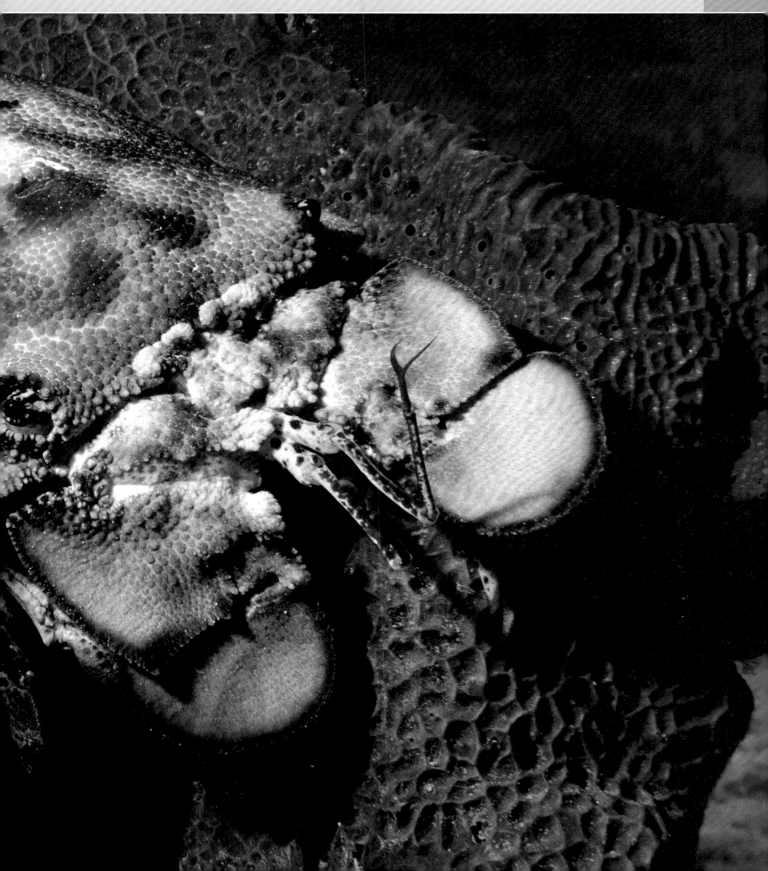

◀ A close up of an Antarctic krill with a stomach full of yellow algae.

Krill tend to live in densely populated swarms and number up to 60,000 in a cubic meter, offering rich pickings for predators. A single blue whale can consume a ton of krill in a gulp – and may feed as many as four times a day. A habit of vertical migration between the depths and the ocean's surface undertaken regularly by krill gives all manner of creatures a chance to feast on them.

Copepods

To catch a copepod it takes a fine net, to identify one a microscope. Although some are visible to the naked eye many more are not. And even under magnification it can be far from clear which species is in the spotlight. In ten subclasses, there are over 240 described families, 2,600 genera and over 21,000 described species.

Single-eyed crustaceans, the name copepod means 'oarfeet' in Greek and it refers to the large hind attachments of some species.

▼ This krill swarm off the California coast provides a rich feeding ground for larger marine inhabitants.

Krill

Filter feeders that thrive on zooplankton, krill (Euphausiacea) only measure between 3 and 6 cm (2 in) but are an enormously important part of the ocean eco-system. Krill constitutes the main part of the diet of numerous whales, seals, penguins and many fish. When krill populations collapse those creatures are left to starve. As many krill feed from algae beneath the polar ice, climate change could pose a significant threat, and they are also vulnerable to parasites.

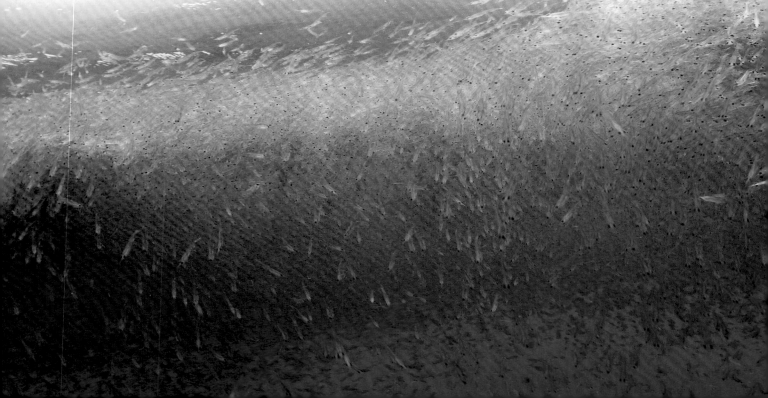

By far the largest group of small crustaceans, copepods are the dominant force among zooplankton. Without these tiny creatures, that usually measure between 1 and 5 mm (less than one quarter of an inch) numerous fish species, as well as whales, sharks and birds would quite simply waste away.

As for copepods themselves, they feed on phytoplankton and detritus although there are a couple of predator species for whom fellow copepods make an ideal meal. Some species will band together and cripple a small fish by devouring its fins. Once it is helpless in the water they will turn their attentions to its body.

Copepods devour the larvae of mosquitoes, which helps to reduce malaria. However, some species are internal or external parasites.

They are found not just in the sunlit zone – there are species that live at far greater depths in the deep sea. Often various species will join the wide-ranging vertical migration that happens at twilight and dawn in the oceans.

Male copepods tend to be smaller than females and less numerous. They form tiny pods of sperm that are transferred to a female by thoracic appendages and are cemented to her body for fertilization before being released into the open sea.

▶ *Copepods such as this are a vital ingredient in the marine food cycle.*

One key to the rampant success of the copepod may have been uncovered by researchers in Denmark who revealed in 2010 that copepods are the world's best animal jumpers, achieving 500 body lengths per second. They are powered by miniscule muscles around their jointed appendages and kick off in the water, rather than from rocks or the ocean floor. The revelation was made after researchers used a high-speed digital camera to track a copepod jump. It is now thought this is how they escape capture and so continue to proliferate.

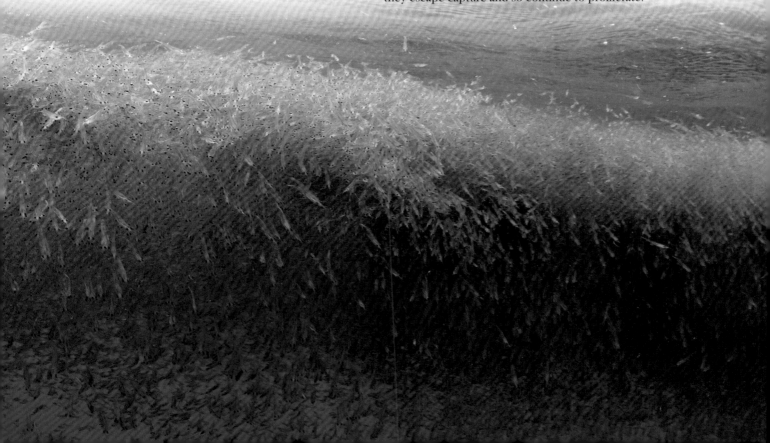

Chelicerates

The more primitive of the arthropod groups, it includes horseshoe crabs and sea spiders. These are animals with six pairs of appendages, one of which, the chelicerae, is modified for feeding.

▲ *A group of horseshoe crabs at high tide during spawning at Cape May, New Jersey.*

Horseshoe crabs

Inside the shell of a horseshoe crab (Xiphosura) is a crescent body in three distinct regions: the cephalothorax, the abdomen and the telson. The cephalothorax is sufficiently large to provide a base for the appendages. The abdomen is smaller and is the site for the gills. The telson is a long spike with dual purpose: to fend off enemies and to steer.

Horseshoe crabs swim, by flexing the abdomen, and walk. They are nocturnal feeders who favor worms, mollusks and algae. Using their chelicerae, they grasp food and pass it to the walking legs behind. At their joint with the cephalothorax, the walking legs have a device to crush the food which is then passed to the mouth for consumption.

During the mating season the smaller male horseshoe crabs attach themselves to the shell of a female, either singly or in numbers. She then heads to shore on a high tide to lay her eggs in the sand and the males are on hand to add their sperm. She will cover the eggs before swimming back to sea, leaving them to heat in the sun. The larvae that hatch are carried back to the ocean by a subsequent high tide.

Sea spiders

With spindly legs and a slight body, sea spiders (Pycnogonida) live in both intertidal and deep waters, including the polar seas. Their size also encompasses a broad range, from a few millimeters to 75 cm (2 ft 6 in).

Usually they have four pairs of walking legs but some species have five or even six, extending to roughly seven times the length of its body. Their bodies are restricted to two sections, the cephalothorax and the abdomen.

Its exoskeleton is non calcareous, made instead of three layers of endocuticle, one of which being sufficiently flexible to support free movement. On its back there is an eye turret, containing four simple eyes, that gives the animal a perception of its environment. If it didn't look odd enough already it also has a proboscis which adds enzymes to soft-bodied prey and then sucks the juices up into the gut.

Male sea spiders also have segmented ovigerous legs, used for grooming and cleaning until they become essential in the reproduction process. Initially they are used for courtship and then – a rarity in the animal kingdom – it is the male who carries the fertilized eggs around on the appendage until they hatch into larvae. First the male gathers the eggs released into the sea by the female after depositing sperm on them. He doesn't restrict himself to the eggs of one partner either and he may collect balls of eggs from ten or more.

▶ *A Pycnogonid or sea spider makes its precarious way across anchor ice in Antarctica.*

BONY FISH

An extraordinary diversity exists beneath the waves, making the study of oceans so compelling. Such is the breadth of life in the deep - from animals to have survived since prehistoric times to recently found specimens - it is taxing to describe them other than in broad brush strokes. Even among creatures that we might clump together as fish there are marked differences. In fact, scientists categorise fish in three types: bony, cartilaginous and jawless. The most prolific in number are bony fish, a family that includes tuna, eels and sea horses. Although they bear certain resemblances to big fish like tuna and cod, the classification excludes sharks, stingrays and dolphins. (The first two are cartilaginous fish and the third is a cetacean.)

About 400 million years ago it was the 'age of the fishes'. From jawless creatures which had ruled the waves evolved fish with paired fins, skeletons made of calcium phosphates and carbonates (which together form bone), scales, a pair of gills, nostrils and recognizable jaws.

The gills help the fish to breathe and the jaws to eat as fish need plenty of energy to keep swimming. Some fish swim in short bursts to either eat or avoid being eaten. Others undertake awesomely lengthy migrations across the planet.

To help, bony fish evolved a special swim bladder filled with gas from the blood stream that keeps them buoyant in water without perpetually swimming. Thanks to the swim bladder they neither rise to the surface nor sink to the bottom, effectively becoming weightless in the water. It permits them to stay at the same level in the ocean for several hours without suffering exhaustion. Fish that live primarily at the ocean bottom may find the swim bladder redundant.

Running down the side of their bodies gill to tail there is a lateral line which helps fish sense movement in the water, an early warning system for the presence of food and predators.

◄ *Butterflyfish are specialist eaters feeding mainly on coral reefs, the mouth has evolved into a short tubular snout that enables the fish to poke into tiny crevices in the reef to extract its prey.*

◄ *A close-up in which the lateral line is clearly visible on this cod.*

Fish are at the heart of the ocean's ongoing renewal process. They are either eaten, when their bodies become energy for others, or they die a natural death and sink to the sea bed. There bacteria get to work on the corpse, break it into tiny particles which then flow back into the water to become food for plankton. Of course it is with plankton that the food cycle begins again.

Despite the tactics employed by evolution to make a success of the species, many that were previously abundant have since become extinct. Still, bony fish are by any standards numerous, accounting for 96 per cent of fish species.

Bony fish are collectively known as Class Osteichthyes. They can be found almost everywhere in the world, in salt water and fresh water. There are two subclasses, Actinopterygii, which are ray-finned fishes and Sarcopterygii, lobe finned fishes. The majority of bony fish are ray-finned and are further distinguished by large eyes and no internal nostrils. Lobe-finned or fleshy-finned fish include coelacanth and lungfish and are the fish that developed into amphibians, and then into land-living vertebrates.

Beyond that they are so diverse it is almost impossible to talk in anything but generalities.

No matter which class they are in, bony fish have different shapes that jigsaw with their lifestyle. The archetypal fish body is streamlined and its shape suggests both pace and power. It is properly known as a fusiform body, which is capable of the high speeds necessary to pounce on prey.

Tropical fish are often laterally compressed, with sides pushed together, like angel fish. They are less concerned with outrunning their dinner and more able to slot into narrow crevasses where they might find food and shelter. To counter a comparative lack of speed, many have what is known as disruptive coloration, making them less obvious to predators.

▼ *The great barracuda is a ray-finned fish that is streamlined for speedy attacks.*

Other fish are shorter and wider, pressed from top to bottom, spending most of their day at the ocean floor. This body shape is normally accompanied by camouflage that mimics sand or gravel. Finally there is the elongated shape, most associated with eels, which are clearly built for speed.

Bony fish can be tiny or absolutely immense, and cover every size in between. There are countless hundreds that are very small, perhaps a few centimeters (an inch). The dwarf pygmy goby (*Pandaka pygmaea*), now endangered, will not breach 15 mm (0.6 in).

Meanwhile the longest is the oarfish (*Regalecus glesne*) which can reach a mammoth 11 m (36 ft) in length. It is thought oarfish are at the root of numerous sea monster sightings because of their curling body and horse-like head. Sunfish (*Mola mola*) are the heavyweights of the sea, topping 2,300 kg (5,071 lb).

▲ *A blue-striped angelfish feeds among the coral, always ready to hide from potential danger.*

▶ *Imagine this oarfish at 11 m long and it is easy to see why sailors believed the oceans were inhabited by sea monsters*

Another clue to the lifestyle of each individual fish comes with the shape of its mouth. At a basic level, fish mouths are either large – suitable for eating fish meat – or small, better suited to nibbling plants or much smaller prey.

After that the mouth might be directed upwards, called dorsal, which indicates that the fish eats at the surface. An anterior mouth runs in the same direction as the lateral line and belongs to fish who feed in the open sea. A mouth angled downwards, also known as a ventral mouth, points to a fish that feeds from the ocean floor. Lips are a rarity – mostly fish have hard edges around their mouths.

Beyond this there are species-specific refinements that affect the mouth. Around the mouth of goatfishes (family Mullidae) there are fleshy barbels to help locate food. Butterflyfish have a long, thin snout with which to needle food out of a narrow crevice.

▶ *A longnose butterflyfish, part of the butterflyfish family that is found in reefs in the Atlantic, Indian and Pacific Oceans.*

In fish the tongue lacks importance as water will carry out the task of manipulating food – and that's what we humans depend on the tongue for. Consequently in fish it has evolved to be a rough, largely immobile, pad in the jaw space. Surrounding the tongue is the buccal cavity, from where mucus is released to aid in the swallowing of food.

As for teeth, fish tend to have more of a spread of dentine than we humans. The impressive ranks of teeth that many possess probably evolved from scales. Depending on the species, fish have teeth along the jaws, on the tongue, in the lips and down their throat. Some of the types of teeth that fish have are roughly equivalent to ours, however.

Meat eaters have cone-shaped canines to grip food and rip at it. Sturdy flat-topped molars are more prevalent in fish that feed on the ocean floor and need to crunch into shell-covered mollusks. Sometimes fish molars fuse together to form a plate for more efficient grinding movements. Plant eaters set greater store by their incisors which have the ability to saw through vegetation or may have spade-like teeth for surface-scraping.

Then there are long, fine villiform teeth, ideal for stabbing. Moray eels are proud possessors of teeth in the pharynx that will swing forward like rogue dentures to secure wriggling prey. The teeth then move back into position, taking the unfortunate fish with them down the throat. Fish teeth are polyphyodont, which means they regularly fall out and are swiftly replaced.

Bony fish breathe when water pours into their mouths. The water moves beneath the operculum, the flap which protects the gills, across the gills themselves then passes out the gill slits. In the gills there is a curved structure made of bone or cartilage which support a number of paired filaments. Tiny attachments extending from these filaments, covered by a wafer-thin membrane and in close proximity to blood vessels, are responsible for the process of gas exchange. In effect, oxygen from the water is swapped for carbon dioxide, a waste product from the fish.

Fish have a heart, arteries, veins and capillaries and accordingly appear to have a circulatory system that we ourselves would recognize. However, their blood pressure tends to be low because blood is not returned to the heart after oxygenation. In response to this some fish, including tuna, improve their body heat – and consequently their muscle efficiency and swimming speed – by using a countercurrent heat exchange system. Essentially heat is transferred from oxygenated blood in the arteries to blood in the veins via capillaries. Fish gulp seawater to breathe and for water.

Given the amount of salt water they take aboard it is important that fish have some means by which to rid themselves of excess sodium. Special chloride cells on the gills work to do this and the kidneys and digestive tract also help to eliminate it. As fish need to retain saltless water they produce very little urine.

Internal anatomy

▼ *The swim bladder runs parallel to the spinal cord in this illustration of a fish's internal anatomy.*

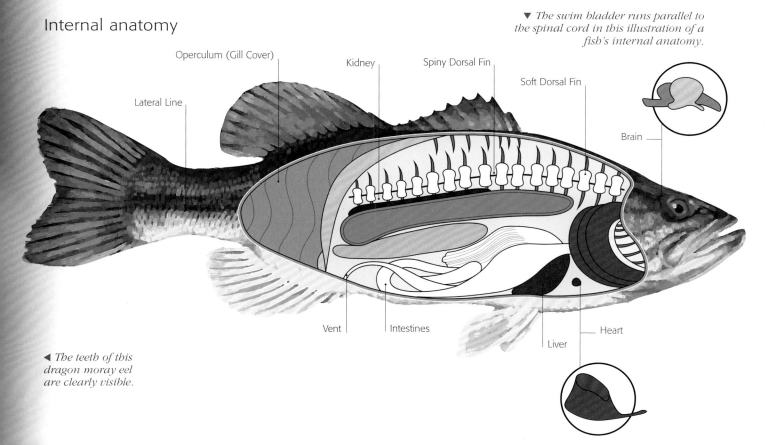

Operculum (Gill Cover)

Kidney

Spiny Dorsal Fin

Soft Dorsal Fin

Lateral Line

Brain

Vent

Intestines

Liver

Heart

◄ *The teeth of this dragon moray eel are clearly visible.*

Fins

All fish have fins, designed to stabilize them in the water. It is the difference between the types of fins that sets the two classes of bony fish apart. Although the fins of ray-finned fish are not bony they can be spiny. In other species fins are soft. Both types are modified forms of scales and are considerably smaller than the fins of their ancestors.

The dorsal fin, usually found on the back, helps to stop the fish rolling and helps it to turn as it swims. Catfish (*order Siluriformes*) can lock the dorsal fin at its maximum spread, deterring attackers and also creating a useful anchor among rocks in a current. Meanwhile anglerfish (*order Lophiiformes*) use the dorsal fin to lure prey. The first section of their dorsal fin is separate and rides high above its body in the water, like a radio mast, assuming the proportions of possible prey for passing fish. The hunter then becomes the hunted as the anglerfish's mighty jaws snap into action.

External Anatomy

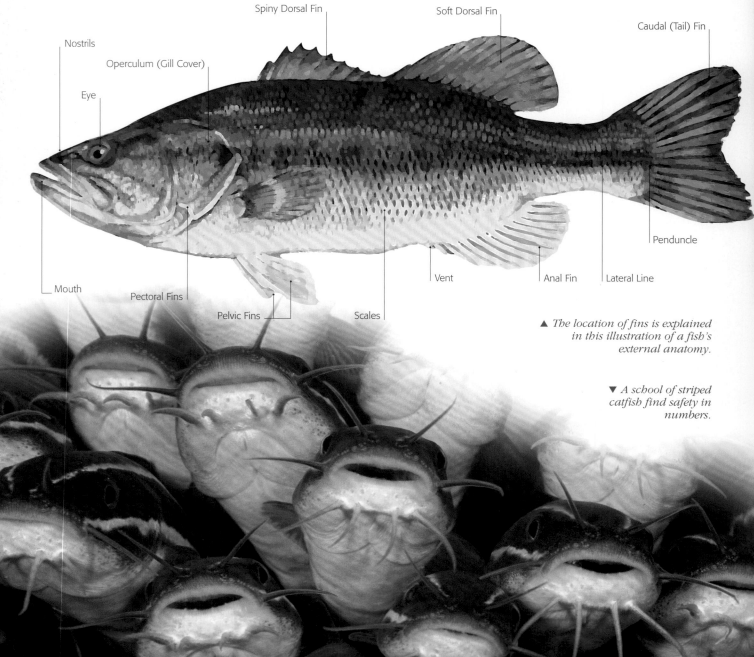

Spiny Dorsal Fin

Soft Dorsal Fin

Caudal (Tail) Fin

Nostrils

Operculum (Gill Cover)

Eye

Penduncle

Mouth

Pectoral Fins

Pelvic Fins

Scales

Vent

Anal Fin

Lateral Line

▲ *The location of fins is explained in this illustration of a fish's external anatomy.*

▼ *A school of striped catfish find safety in numbers.*

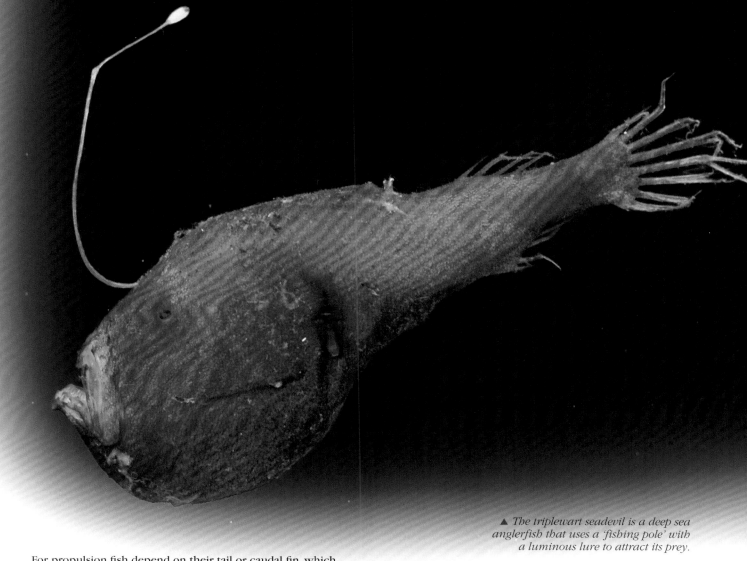

▲ *The triplewart seadevil is a deep sea anglerfish that uses a 'fishing pole' with a luminous lure to attract its prey.*

For propulsion fish depend on their tail or caudal fin, which comes in different and distinct shapes. In strictly layman's terms they can appear like an arrow head, a torpedo nose, a flattened spatula, a half moon, a trowel or asymmetrical.

Another stabilizing device, the anal fin, is located to the rear of the fish on its underside while the paired pectoral fins are on each side.

For some fish it is the combination of two or more fins that defines their existence. Flying fish (Exocoetidae) swing their tails – as much as 70 times per second – then spread and tilt their unusually long pectoral fins to achieve uplift. After that they can exit the water with graceful style. Before re-entering the water, flying fish draw in their pectoral fins and drop their tails. Thanks to their hard-working fins flying fish can achieve distances of up to 150 m (492 ft) during 20 seconds of air time. It is an effective way to elude water-bound predators

Other species, including anglerfish and mudskippers (family Periophthalmidae), use their pectoral fins as feet, to 'walk' or 'stand' on the ocean floor.

Below the pectoral fins lie the pelvic or ventral fins, which help to control movement and are useful brakes.

Some fish have an extra one, the adipose fin which is soft and fleshy and lies behind the dorsal fin in species like salmon and catfish. In addition there are finlets, generally behind the dorsal and anal fins and used for extra balance. Fast swimmers also might have a caudal keel in front of the tail fin for extra streamlining.

Evolution has cost some species their fins, particularly the moray eels which lack pectoral and pelvic fins. The anal fin is absent from other species.

▲ *Rainbowfish – such as these from the Goyder River – live in a wide range of freshwater habitats, including rivers, lakes, and swamps.*

Scales

Fish scales tucked up in the dermis provide protection. But a fish that's protected with heavy armor pays a price in terms of speed and agility. Meanwhile the nimble fishes that dart from rock to cave have thinner, less fortified skin that puts them at risk from both predators and accidental damage. Nor are scales compulsory for fish, with sunfish a prime example of a species that flourishes without them.

Scales are not uniform in size, with some measured by the centimeter and others by the millimeter or are even more microscopic still. Fast-moving fish are more likely to have small scales, which best suit a rapid body action. However, some fish compensate for the need for speed by having larger scales near the largely immobile head, decreasing in size until much smaller ones cover the active tail.

In bony fish there are three different types of scales. Tough cosmoid scales, which were effectively layered bone, have

been lost to extinction. The coelacanth has modified cosmoid scales, though, which lack the robust outer layer and are consequently much thinner than the originals.

Ganoid scales are similar to the archaic cosmoid ones but have a different construction, featuring enamel. They are diamond shaped, shiny and remain extremely durable.

However, it is usually leptoid scales, made from calcium and tissue, that adorn the skins of bony fish, growing in concentric layers and overlapping like roof tiles. There are two forms of leptoid scale. The first, cycloid scales, have a smooth outer edge and are usually found on fish with soft fin rays. On spiny fin rays it is more common to find ctenoid scales which are dog-tooth shaped.

But these wide-ranging categories incorporate numerous variations. Some scales have modified into spines some of

▲ *Yellow-tailed surgeonfish (Prionurus laticlavius) school, Wolf Island, Galapagos Islands, Ecuador*

which are razor-sharp, as with surgeon fish. Scales with sharp, raised edges called scutes provide even better protection than the norm.

Herring and anchovies are two examples of fish with what are known as deciduous scales, which are easily shed during pursuit or near capture. Sometimes the scales stack up around the lateral line to assist in protection.

What were once scales on sea horses and pipe fish have evolved into a tiny suit of armor, which hinders movement. In boxfish the armor is so complete it acts something like a shell. Rings on fish scales are used as a pointer to the age of fish. Using this method it is thought that some large fish can live up to 80 years.

▶ *The longhorn boxfish and other family members are notable for the hexagonal or 'honeycomb' patterns in their skin and skeletons.*

Reproduction

Given the vast numbers of bony fish in existence it is hardly surprising that there are numerous methods of reproduction. Cod (Gadidae), tuna (Scombridae) and sardines (Clupeidae) are pelagic spawners, meaning the females release vast quantities of eggs into the water where they are duly fertilized by males then left to drift. Fish eggs contain an oil which is lighter than water to help them disperse over a wide area. This spreads the population but, with the eggs so vulnerable, means many are lost before they even hatch. To counter this, pelagic spawners tend towards a lengthy period of fertility.

Benthic spawners, such as smelt (Osmeridae), who live closer to the shore, produce eggs without buoyancy. The eggs, lodged in rocks or among seaweed, have a large yolk to help nourish the larvae. Later the hatchling might stay in the vicinity or head off to the open sea.

Then there are a group known as brood hiders. Fish like the grunion (*leuresthes tenuis*) secretes its eggs out of sight but thereafter provides no parental care. At a high tide under a full moon grunion swim towards shore and the female burrows in the sand in order to lay her eggs. Males coil themselves around their mates so they can fertilize the eggs as they are laid. The grunions disappear back to sea, leaving the eggs in the sand. They won't be liberated until the next high tide, when they are hatched and sucked back out to sea.

There are some fish that exhibit mothering instincts, though, and care for their offspring in the early stages. Some species of damselfish (Pomacentridae), blennies (Blennioidei) and gobies (Gobiidae) will prepare a nest – or sometimes plump for a bare surface – to lay eggs. The eggs are then guarded by the males until they are hatched, a waiting time which extends from a few days to a few months. With some species the care continues in the larval stage.

▼ *A sergeant major group guard the nests of eggs laid around the base of a large bommie of hard coral.*

Jawfish (*Opistognathus macrognathus*) and seahorses are examples of fish that bear live youth. The male jawfish keeps eggs in his mouth until they hatch while seahorses have a special pouch.

Meanwhile many fish are hermaphrodites, both male and female, thus increasing the potential of young.

It is not an easy life for a larva, being swept up with the ranks of plankton and vulnerable to almost every other ocean dweller who chooses to feast on it. Some species of larvae are helped by a yolk sac attached to their abdomen which is eventually absorbed, helping them to develop. A larva must ride its luck until it is fully developed. The number of larvae initially hatched for outweights the number that survive until adulthood, which is why it is essential that they are born in great numbers.

▶ *A male jawfish protectively incubates a clutch of eggs in his mouth.*

▼ *Atlantic salmon larvae with yolk-sacs; in a few days they will begin hunting tiny invertebrates.*

▲ *While many blind cave fish are born without eyes, the cave dwelling Mexican tetra's eyes quickly degenerate due to lack of use and become covered in skin.*

Communication

Fish have various means of communication, including movement, posing and coloration. They also use sound, by grinding their teeth and making their swim bladder vibrate. There's a third option too, which involves releasing intoxicating chemicals called pheromones into the water, which can inspire various responses in others of the same species, thought to be able to detect them by smell.

For some fish, their sense of smell is what leads them to their next meal. The olfactory receptors of bony fish are found in pits that are washed by water during swimming or via a constriction of the nasal sacs. Fish that depend greatly on their sense of smell have elongated sacs and receptors

Fish who live in the shallows where light is plentiful usually have small eyes. Those who prefer the depths tend towards large eyes that will enable them to absorb as much of the scarce sunrays as possible. A few have a reflective layer behind their eyes that reflects the light through the retina a second time, making the most of what little light penetrates the deeper ocean. Most fish are not endowed with the ability to dilate their pupils nor do they have eyelids.

With eyes generally placed on each side of the head their field of vision ahead is narrow and to the side, monocular.

As always with bony fish, it is difficult to talk specifics. Goldfish, for example, are known to have fine eyesight, being able to distinguish objects some 4.8 m (15.7 ft) distant. Other types, like cavefish, are entirely blind, using sharpened senses other than sight to survive. The blind goby is born with eyes that disappear as the fish matures.

◀ *Four-eyed fish have eyes raised above the top of the head and divided in two different parts, so that they can see below and above the water surface at the same time.*

More curious still, flat fish like flounder are born with eyes each side of their head, only to have one eye migrate towards the other to suit their adult lifestyle lying low on a sandy ocean floor.

Oddly, there is a family of bony fish at home in the river mouths around South America that has its claim to fame on eyesight issues. The four-eyed fish in fact only has two eyes but each is divided horizontally so that it can check out what's happening above and below the water at the same time. As this is a fish that prefers to swim at the surface and snack on insects on top of the water as well as small fish below it is an ideal quality to have developed. It also has the advantage over predators, with one part of each eye looking to see what's coming.

Some species, including puffer fish, are primarily dependent on their eyes for locating prey.

▼ *A close-up of the white-spotted puffer, often found in areas of sea grass in reefs, lagoons, estuaries, and tidal pools.*

Although they don't have ear holes, fish can hear as sound travels through soft tissues to reach the inner ear. Sometimes the swim bladder is strategically close to the ear to enhance the reception of sound. Although they don't have the same hearing range as humans, fish can detect sounds in the range of 200 to 13,000 hertz. Most fish are thought to hear prey before they see it.

The lateral line also senses vibrations much like the ear. Running down each side of the fish, it disguises a series of fluid-filled channels which contain sensory cells. Small fibers on the cells can detect water turbulence, currents or other vibrations at large in the water. The fish is then alerted, through the sensory cells, to possible danger.

Taste receptors of bony fish can be found on their heads, jaws, tongues, mouths and barbells that protrude from the mouth. Their purpose is not only to detect food but also to distinguish toxins.

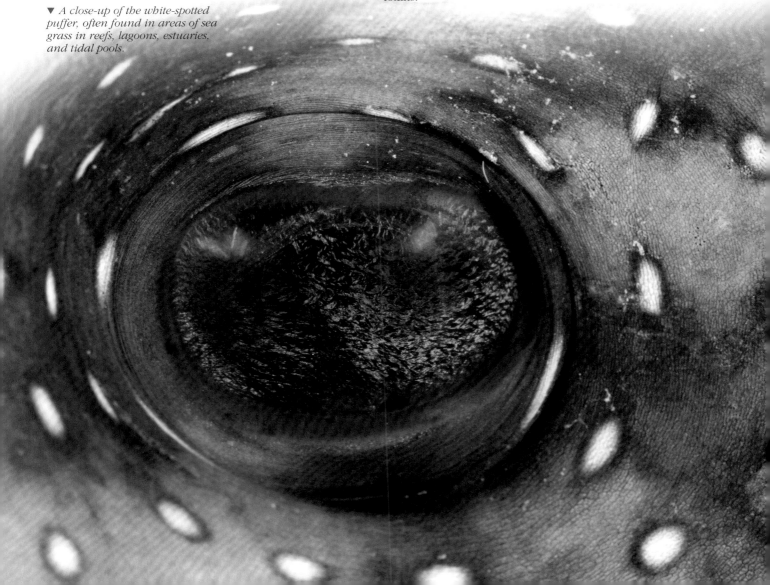

Schools

In the open ocean there is no place to hide; no rocky crevice to hole up in and no forest of seaweed to use as camouflage. The ocean surface is ruthlessly exposed while the sea bed is inaccessibly distant. It is no place to be alone. Gatherings of fish in large groups in the middle of the sea to migrate or follow their food supply are called schools. And if there's one lesson that fish have learned from this underwater school it is that there is safety in numbers.

Schools differ from shoals as they are single-species and they can be impressively large. One school of herring was measured at 4.5 million cubic meters (159 million cubic feet).

Off African shores between May and July millions of one sardine variety, pilchard *Sardinops*, swarm towards Mozambique before heading off into the Indian Ocean in the wake of a specific and fruitful cold water current. The water boils in an underwater cloud that measures some 7 km (4.5 miles) long, 1.5 km (0.9 miles) wide and 30 m (98 ft) deep. A major tourist attraction, it is an incredible sight to behold as it can clearly be observed from above the waterline. Sometimes the run fails to occur, which is bad news for the local fisherman and the shark, dolphin and gannet population who benefit from it.

Together in a school, fish have more chance of detecting incoming predators and less chance of being eaten. The opportunities of finding a mate are also increased. Swimming

▼ *An Atlantic spotted dolphin looks to pick off stragglers from a school of Snappers.*

▶ *A grey reef shark feeds on a large baitfish ball in the South Pacific.*

in a synchronized manner, the fish forage for abundant food supplies in conditions of enhanced safety. The system is not perfect, however.

Anchovies gather in schools measuring hundreds of meters across on the Patagonian shelf off Argentina after cold, nutrient-rich waters are whipped up by the Falklands current. Unfortunately for them, the school becomes a shoal as it is joined by scores of predators, who themselves attract the attention of hungry hunters further up the food chain. Soon it is a feeding frenzy.

Predators confronted by a vast school of fish will only be able to pick off a proportion, given the speed at which schools can change direction with thousands of fish instinctively moving as one.

To counter this sharks and dolphins have developed herding techniques, beating their tales to keep the fish contained in an ever-smaller space close to the ocean's surface. The result is what is known as a bait-ball, in which the prey is more concentrated and the feed for the predator more satisfying.

Migration

The migration of fish from one part of the ocean to some far distant river bed is a miracle of nature. The navigational feat that takes particular fish to their designated spawning grounds is, to date, inexplicable. But the power of these unseen ties is relentless and draws the fish as if by magic across thousands of hazardous miles. The reward for the trek is reproduction rights.

Of course, fish don't go-it-alone on this mysterious journey. Before it begins they tend to congregate, presumably awaiting a signal from time or tide. Many fish schools might come together for migration, uniting to start their 'run' up a river. Nor do all species clamor to get underway at the same time. Whitefish begin their run in the autumn while carp and other species start in the spring.

When the fish are traveling from oceans and seas into rivers it is called anadromous migration. Salmon and sturgeon migrate in this fashion. In reverse, when fish swim from rivers into the sea to spawn, it is called catadromous migration and eels are perhaps the best known for this.

Migration doesn't always happen on such a grand scale, however. Many species spawn in particular areas – among sea grasses or mangroves for example – relatively close to their usual hunting grounds so their journey is short.

Nor is all migration horizontal. As we know, the vertical migration between the depths of the ocean and the sunlit zone during the twilight hours is carried out on a colossal scale. This is primarily done so that creatures can feed in fertile grounds under cover of darkness. But some species also head for the surface to spawn, their larvae then numbering among the hosts of zooplankton that swarm in those warmer waters. It is a process that also happens in reverse, with creatures whose natural habitat is close to the top of the ocean heading for the depths to reproduce.

Also, migration occurs with the movement of phytoplankton. As it drifts in the seas it is pursued by its predators, who in turn are followed by bigger species. And some species head for deep water in winter to escape the turbulence of storms in a seasonal migration. Every winter a staggering eight billion Atlantic herring are believed to squeeze in the deep, sheer-sided fjords of Norway, where they are protected from the worst of the winter weather. Unfortunately for them, killer whales tend to be hot on their tails.

▼ Sockeye salmon attempt to negotiate a fast flowing waterfall in Alaska.

Generally, migration is not a time for food or rest. Having stocked up on body fat it is a case of heading hell for leather to the spawning grounds. Sockeye salmon travel up to 40 km (25 miles) a day while for chum salmon the distance covered is even greater. Scientists have discovered that Atlantic salmon heading through the White Sea when they are immature do take time out to feed. It slows their progress so much that fully developed Atlantic salmon who embark on their journey in the spring may even catch up with the fall leavers.

Every obstacle from rock to waterfall takes its toll on fish that grow ever more exhausted with each passing day. It is vital that after spawning they return to a salt water environment as quickly as possible.

The store of body fat that fuels the fish diminishes as the trek goes on. And for the female fish heading up river the eggs she is carrying increase her load. Nature compensates by giving female fish greater reserves of fat in the first place although she will end up with a lower fat ratio than a male in the long term.

Although creatures like the sockeye salmon (*Oncorhynchus nerka*), who migrate distances of 3,600 km (2,237 miles), earn our undying admiration there's inevitably a price to be paid and for them it is costly indeed. Having spawned up river, the physical demands of the journey take their toll and the fish are unable to swim back down to the sea. They die in the river where they were born and gave birth.

It is not the same sorry tale for Atlantic salmon *(Salmo salar)* as the distances involved are much less. While a journey of 400 km (250 miles) is not to be sneezed at, it does leave the fish with some reserves, enough for the journey down river to the sea. They live to spawn another day and will repeat the arduous trip within a few years, spawning three or four times before they die.

Smell could play a part in the migratory process, so might magnetic forces that spiral around the earth. Beyond that we can only surmise that fish memory-map the journey as juveniles with pin sharp accuracy. This indeed would be astonishing as they return not just to the neighborhood but to the exact spot where they were born.

Fish senses relate directly back to the brain which is essentially divided into three. The forebrain deals with the ability of bony fish to pick up scent. Creatures with particularly acute sense of smell, like the eel, will have a bigger forebrain by comparison with others.

The midbrain is associated with sight, learning and response. Fish with keen eyesight are likely to be well endowed in the midbrain while it might wither for those who are short sighted or blind. The hindbrain is linked to movement and muscle tone and the fast movers are likely to have the most correspondingly large brain section here.

▲ *Atlantic salmon typically migrate from their home stream and an area on the continental plate off west Greenland.*

▶ *Sockeye salmon are blue tinged with silver in color while living in the ocean but both sexes turn red with green heads and sport a dark stripe on their sides prior to spawning.*

Food

Bony fish can be carnivores, feasting on the flesh of other fish; herbivores, relishing the underwater plant life and possibly aided by a gizzard to help grind the food; omnivores, eating meat and plants; or what are known as detritivores, creatures that enjoy rotting meat and plants. Anchovies are filter feeders, straining plankton from water with gill rakers. Meanwhile some species of bony fish, like the cleaner wrasse (*Labroides dimidiatus*), pick up their food from larger fish whose bodies are troubled with parasites.

Creatures most commonly targeted by bony fish are crustaceans, annelid snails, mussels, squid, small mammals and, of course, other fish.

However, there are some finely honed features on bony fish to help them go in for the kill. Some fish, including the electric catfish (*Malapterurus electricus*), produce an electric current to stun their prey.

The archerfish (*Toxotes jaculatrix*) fires missiles at insects flying above the water, felling them from heights of 1.8 m (5.9 ft). When the insect body lies inert on the ocean's surface it becomes instantly accessible. Equally well armed, the swordfish (*Xiphias gladius*) has a long, sharp bill that it uses to thrash and slash through a school of smaller fish, eating the dead or injured afterwards. Given that it is a swift swimmer, the carnage it can inflict is immense.

Lying undetected on the ocean floor, thanks to its superb camouflage, the energy-conscious stone fish (*Synanceja* spp.) simply waits for dinner to swim by and then pounces. Perhaps unexpectedly, small fish, especially those from warmer climates, tend to eat more pound for pound than large fish. This is because they generally have a higher metabolic rate. At the other end of the spectrum, some varieties of eel can last a year without food.

Fish colors

Color among fish species is used to both conceal and to attract attention. It comes from pigment in fish cells or light-reflecting, iridescent crystals near their skins.

Perhaps the most brightly colored fish are those haunting the coral reefs. It is thought that the striking patterns of tropical fish may be linked to territorial rights, sexual displays or may even help with foraging.

Disruptive coloration is also a feature among tropical fish, with broad, vertical lines or dark spots playing a visual trick on predators who might fail to see a fish outline because of it. Fish that live in the open ocean depend on countershading as a way of evading predators. That means their backs are

▼ *This stone scorpionfish is almost indiscernible from the ocean bed as it patiently awaits its next meal.*

dark colored, so from a high level aspect they blend with the depths of the ocean. Meanwhile their guts are silvery, so anything looking up at them from below would have difficulty making them out against the brightness of the ocean surface.

Cryptic coloring is another word for camouflage, when fish merge into the background by adopting the same colors and tones as their surroundings. Masters of this are the flat fish, whose bodies are the color of sand. They lie on an ocean bed undetected until prey happens along, unnoticed by passing predators.

Defensive systems

One sure-fire way to confuse a passing predator is to light up like a Christmas decoration. This is a technique some species use to their advantage. Called bioluminescence, it tends to occur in deeper waters where there is no natural light to dilute the effect. Bioluminescence happens in various organs or in special cells called photophores through a chemical reaction. It is sometimes not the fish that lights up but bacteria in or on it. The most prevalent color is blue or green, colors that travel the furthest in the ocean. However some fish favor red, infrared or even yellow light. It is, of course, how lantern fish and flashlight fish got their names. Their abiding hope is that the light decorating the length of their bodies will confuse natural enemies. Apart from deterring its enemies a fish might use bioluminescence to see in the dark, lure prey or to attract a mate.

The puffer fish (*Arothron hispidus*) is able to gulp water in order to swell up to twice its normal size and looks like a ball. Although it slows swimming speed, the aim is to deter possible predators and few could get their jaws around a puffer fish when its elastic skin is fully stretched. It has a close relative, the porcupine fish, who uses the same expansive technique with the refinement of extending spines that normally lie flat on its side. It is enough to alarm and repel the vast majority of attackers.

Any creature with its predatory gaze on a puffer fish would be well advised to move away as its internal organs contain deadly quantities of a paralyzing poison called tetrodotoxin, reputedly 1,200 times more lethal than cyanide. It has got the better of many Japanese diners who see puffer fish as a delicacy despite the dangers and the fact that chefs preparing the dish must be licensed.

▲ *A myriad of shades as tropical fish and coral combine to provide a cacophony of color.*

Clown fish (genus *Amphiprion*) have made a friend of poisonous sea anemones to help keep their enemies at bay. They live among anemone tentacles, an environment that would be dangerous if not deadly to its predators. No one is sure why clown fish are tolerated by sea anemones that would normally make short work of a creature so close. It is possible the clown fish secretes a mucus that effectively keeps it safe. In return for this protection, the clown fish keeps its sea anemone clean by eating detritus among the swaying tentacles, including fish parts left over from the anemone's last meal.

The surgeonfish (*Acanthurus olivaceus*) is armed with scalpel-sharp blades to fend off predators. It has a pair of spines located on the sides of its tail which it snaps out much like a switchblade in times of crisis.

▼ *Note the light pores near the tail of this Lanternfish which are designed to confuse predators.*

Sun fish

Among the most absurd looking fish in the seas, the ocean sunfish (*Mola mola*) has a short dorsal fin, long anal fins and a crescent tail. With such a quaint body shape it must squirt out a jet of water from its mouth or gills in order to steer. Primarily made of cartilage they boast just 16 vertebrae. Nonetheless, they can achieve enormous dimensions and have tipped the scales at two tonnes (2.2 US tons).

Their behavior is sometimes as remarkable as their appearance. Something of a target for parasites which can latch on despite the fish's tough skin, individuals will seek out a halfmoon perch to act as its cleaner. During the process of cleaning the sunfish will suspend itself almost vertically in the water to permit the cleaners maximum access.

If there is no halfmoon perch on hand then they head to the surface and attract the attention of passing gulls which will obligingly peck away at the offending parasites. Clearly, the sunfish would be too much for a single gull to handle but there still seems an element of risk in this behavior.

◄ *Sunfish are not equipped with a swim bladder and as a result use their fins much like a bird uses its wings.*

Coelacanths

Coelacanths (*Latimeria chalumnae*) have proved to be among nature's great survivors. Initially known only from fossil records, early marine biologists assumed the species was among the ranks of the extinct until one was caught by a fisherman from East London, South Africa, in 1938.

With its substantial scales and ill-defined tail, it certainly looked like a species that would have been well-fitted to life 80 million years ago. For a while it was tempting to think this was a sole survivor. However, another specimen was caught in the Indian Ocean in 1952, the first of several. Then, in 1998, a new species of coelacanth was fished out of the sea off the Indonesian coast when scientists had no idea that finding *Latimeria menadoensis* was even on the cards.

A deep sea dweller, the coelacanth has a skeleton of both bone and cartilage, which helps to ease movement in its heavy, bony jacket.

◄ *One of the most enduring fish in the oceans, coelacanth sightings are very rare.*

Parrotfish

As the name suggests, parrot fish (Scaridae) are brightly colored and have a beak-like mouth which is in fact a fusion of continuously-growing teeth. With this they scrape the algae from the coral in their tropical habitats, although they are not necessarily vegetarians. This feeding habit can sometimes scar the reef for considerable periods.

At night they wedge themselves into a rocky crevice, often covering themselves with slime to disguise their scent and perhaps anchor them to the spot. After eating bits of rock and coral, parrotfish excrete sand in significant amounts. It is thought one of the larger parrotfish species can produce 90 kg (200 lbs) of sand each year. They are close relatives of the wrasse.

In most parrotfish species fish begin as females but turn into males before they die. This unorthodox lifestyle is accompanied by wide-ranging color changes.

▲ The distinctive beak of the species is clearly visible on this blue-barred parrotfish.

Seahorses

Given its vertical stance and equine head, the seahorse (*Hippocampus*) looks far removed from the fish with which it shares the oceans. But these endearing creatures are just as much bony fish as cod and salmon.

There are about 50 different species of seahorse inhabiting weedy sea beds in warm water. Some are under a centimeter long while others extend to 30 cm (12 inches). All have a rigid covering made from scales which have evolved into a shell-like plate. With an odd shape and only tiny fins – a dorsal fin and pectoral fins that are sited behind its eyes- it is not surprising to learn that sea horses are slow swimmers. They compensate for this with an ability to camouflage themselves using a change of color, making themselves invisible to passing predators. Perhaps the most remarkable in the range is the Australian sea horse, which takes the art of camouflage to a new level, by having leaf-like tissue on its body.

Sea horses feed after winding their tail around a reed to await prey that includes shrimp, small fish and plankton. Also, their eyes move independently of one another, in reptilian fashion.

Although it is the female seahorse who produces eggs they are held inside the male's body until they hatch. She ejects her eggs into his empty pouch after an enduring courtship display. He is, to all intents and purposes, pregnant for between 40 and 50 days. Seahorses are the only species to experience this kind of gender confusion.

Sea horses are closely related to pipe fish, although the latter swim in a more typical fashion.

▼ A spotted seahorse male who has just 'given birth' to his offspring.

Billfish

Like an echo from the prehistoric past, billfish scythe through the oceans, the proud bearers of a bony spear protruding from their upper jaws that can measure in excess of a meter (3 ft). There are 11 species of billfish, the largest being the blue marlin (*Makaira nigricans*) which can weigh in at more than 900 kg (1990 lbs) and the fastest being the sailfish, achieving speeds of 110 kph (68 mph). The best known is probably the aptly named swordfish (*Xiphias gladius*).

The spear helps to streamline the bodies of the billfish which, like tuna, have few scales, fins that tuck down and keels and finlets on their tails to reduce drag in the water. Both have large, high tails with molded tips to assist propulsion and they are muscle-bound fish.

As well as benefitting from a circulatory counter current in which heat is exchanged between arteries and veins, swordfish, which are deep water hunters, have specially warmed muscles that warm the blood flowing to their eyes and brains to get maximum performance from their bodies.

▶ *Swordfish can tolerate temperatures of five degrees Celsius and dive to 650 m.*

Fish at risk – Pacific salmon

More than merely food, the Pacific wild salmon has played a role in the culture, faith and livelihood of the native American people. Its decline is all the more poignant for that.

There are five species of Pacific salmon, which are chinook, chum, sockeye, coho and pink. The largest of them is the chinook, which weighs up to 14 kg (31 lb) while the smallest is the pink salmon, usually tipping the scales at no more than 1.8 kg (4 lb). Each of these species has several runs, each returning to its native stream after it has achieved sexual maturity at sometime between the ages of one and five.

Before it leaves the ocean a Pacific salmon may have covered as much as 4,800 km (2,983 miles) in its astonishing feat of endurance. The death rate is uncomfortably high. Only one out of a thousand salmon may survive to spawn in the stream where it was itself hatched.

A female salmon uses her tail to scrape a shallow hole called a redd in which she lays a clump of orange or red colored eggs. An observant male nearby will immediately swim over to add his sperm or milt to the mix. The fertilized eggs are covered in gravel by the female fish, once again using her tail. This happens as many as seven times, with the female laying up to 5,000 eggs at each site.

The outlook is bleak for the Pacific salmon. Recent figures point to more than 100 stocks being lost to extinction. Others are teetering on the brink of collapse.

Among the perils is virulent disease that begins with closely-packed farmed stocks but quickly spreads to wild varieties which have little immunity. Sea lice from the same source also pose immense difficulties. A change in the temperature of oceans and rivers wreaks havoc with the essential body clock of the salmon, putting it under further stress during migration. Salmon also have overfishing, pollution, a shortage of beaver-built pools (caused by a shortage of beavers) and the existence of dams with which to contend.

Dams, which are increasingly vital power sources for the human population, pose a problem for migrating Pacific salmon. Not only do they bar the way, in some cases, to salmon migration but they have inundated spawning pools. So even salmon who find a way through are unable to deposit their eggs appropriately.

Changing the character of a river, as dam construction tends to do, can make it a happy hunting ground for the salmon's natural predators.

Meanwhile, if the water flow is controlled the fish are exposed to higher than normal temperatures and an environment where disease flourishes.

With environment issues close to the top of the international agenda, steps have been taken to mitigate the effect of dams on migrating fish. Fish ladders, for example, have been included in their design to assist juvenile fish and adults in the migration process and to keep them away from the turbines.

Water released upstream helps to reduce water temperature and improve the health of the salmon. Sometimes young fish are collected from the water and taken downstream by trucks or in barges, avoiding the peril of the dam as they journey downstream to the sea.

Where the threat to salmon is insurmountable the removal of the dam is sometimes considered. Obviously, this is only an option with smaller, less consequential dams.

◄ *The pink salmon or humpback salmon is the smallest and most abundant of the Pacific Salmon family.*

▲ *Recently hatched chum salmon clearly displaying their yolk sacs which provide eraly nourishment in bony fish.*

▼ *A chinook salmon (the largest of the Pacific salmon family) swims upriver to spawn in Alaska.*

Bluefin tuna

The largest of the tuna family, a bluefin tuna (*Thunnus thynnus*) can be as long as a man is tall and weighs 135 kg (300 lbs) or more. The heaviest known, however, weighed in at four times that amount. It has a blue-black color to its upper body and silver below and it is well-traveled. A bluefin tuna tagged off the coast of Japan was caught for a second time almost 11,000 km (6,835 miles) away off the Mexican coast. Another tagged bluefin crossed the Atlantic in just 119 days. Had it been traveling in a straight line it would have covered 65 km (40 miles) a day. But it was surely traveling in haphazard fashion as part of its quest for food.

The bluefin tuna is similar to the southern bluefin tuna – only internal differences set them apart. And both are critically endangered.

Bluefin tuna is highly prized in Japanese cooking as it reputedly makes the best sushi and sashimi. Although Japan is the world's largest consumer, the Mediterranean countries are also keen on using it in cuisine. Prices for bluefin tuna have rocketed as the fish being caught are now fewer and smaller than before.

Conservationists are certain that stocks in the eastern Atlantic Ocean and Mediterranean Sea are about to collapse. Some studies have said that Atlantic bluefin stocks have fallen by about 75 per cent in the past 50 years with 60 per cent of that loss occurring in the past ten years. But plans to impose

▲ *The southern bluefin tuna is typically found in open southern hemisphere waters of all the world's oceans mainly between 30°S to nearly 60°S.*

international restrictions on bluefin tuna fishing have received scant support. There's skepticism that the International Commission for the Conservation of Atlantic Tunas (ICCAT), created in response to earlier fears about the welfare of the species and which currently oversees trade, is making sufficient headway to save the tuna from extinction.

In response the World Worldlife Fund has implored restaurateurs, retailers, chefs and consumers to stop selling, serving, buying and eating it.

Atlantic cod

Once prolific around the North Sea, the Bay of Biscay and the coast of Greenland, the Atlantic cod (Gadus morhua) has become a victim of overfishingm so much so that in the 1990's cod stocks collapsed to 95 per cent lower than it's historical position. Despite regulation curbing the size of catches the populations have failed to recover during the 21st century.

Oil spills

On 20 April 2010 BP's Deepwater Horizon rig exploded in the Gulf of Mexico. With the worst of the damage caused deep underwater it was weeks before a leaking pipeline could be plugged and a massive slick seeped into the Gulf, shaped by currents and winds but moving inexorably towards the shores of Louisiana and Alabama.

It was the effect on the shoreline birds and wildlife that focused most people's minds but the unseen consequences for fish were also devastating, as the bluefin tuna in the Gulf was due to spawn within weeks of the disaster.

Seagrasses that provide food and shelter for literally scores of fish, as well as ocean-going mammals, were blighted. It is an area particularly rich

▶ *Litter can take many different forms; here an abandoned Volkswagen Beetle slowly rots on the ocean floor.*

◀ *The Atlantic cod can grow to 2 m (6 ft 7 in) in length, weigh up to 96 kg (210 lb) and live for 25 years.*

in shrimps, upon which a large industry is based. Only time will tell if there's long term ruination of this eco-system before the oil breaks down naturally in the sea water.

But fish and other ocean-going creatures have more to contend with than isolated oil disasters like this. Indeed, oil spillages in the ocean are everyday occurrences. They happen when rogue freight ships empty their tanks at sea and, although the amounts are small, it remains an ongoing problem.

Sea water may be contaminated by effluent from sewage pipelines. Although toilet and waste products will eventually disintegrate in the sea the process takes time.

Add to that the chemicals that are washed into the sea with the rain that has run down from fields containing sprayed crops.

Then there's litter dumped at sea by ships or strewn on beaches. It takes 80 years or so for plastic to rot to nothing in the sea. Moreover garbage can be harmful to the creatures who live in the oceans, where a carrier bag can resemble a jellyfish but will kill the would-be predator who tries to eat it.

BRYOZOA

Consider a cleaner the size of a pinhead and you are halfway to understanding the nature of bryozoans. In Greek bryo means moss and zoan means animal and that instantly summons up an accurate picture of something that is often seen and little understood.

They are very small aquatic invertebrates that sieve microscopic food particles out of the water, so they are comparable to living filters that clean the surrounding environment. Most live in tropical waters at depths above 100 m (330 ft) but a few types live in polar waters and some upright-growing species are even found deep down in oceanic trenches. At first glance many look like a mossy mat.

Individual bryozoa (phylum Ectoprocta) are about 0.5 mm (0.02 in) long. Some species are solitary animals but most live in large co-dependent, co-operative clone colonies. Within the colonies are thousands of tiny individuals called zooids, each in a box like chamber of its own construction.

The colonies can take on various shapes – bushy, tree-like, fans or cabbage shaped. The *Cheilostomata* species produce a mineralized exoskeleton and can look very like coral but the commonest form develops into a sheet-like cover and grows in a single layer over rocks, seaweed and other surfaces. These can grow up to 50 cm (1.6 ft) in diameter and contain around two million zooids.

As filter feeders bryozoa catch food particles from the water using a retractable circular crown of hollow tentacles lined with cilia, scientifically called a lophophore. They absorb

▼ *Bryozoa or sea mat (Bugula plumosa) anchored to rocky substrate off the coast of the Netherlands.*

▲ *Bryozoa colonies contain a combination of zooids that are in their male and female stages.*

oxygen and then expel carbon dioxide through the body wall and tentacles. The mouth lies in the center of the tentacles and the anus outside it.

Autozooids are responsible for catching food, principally phytoplankton, supplying the non-feeding zooids with nutrients and cleaning away excreta. Meanwhile, zooids fill various roles including defending the colony in times of stress, looking after the hatcheries and so on. Most bryozoa species are sessile but a few use spiny defensive zooids as legs, to slowly move the colony a short distance if their location becomes unsuitable.

Colonies can be as small as 1 cm (0.39 in) across, but the majority average about 10 cm (3.9 in), although some can grow up to 1 m (3.3 ft) in diameter. They can grow by asexual budding in a single zooid called the ancestrula that is distinguished by its rounded shape. The colony can live for anything between 1 and 12 years and grows fastest in areas of gently moving currents. Budding seems to be initiated by rising water temperatures in spring when higher levels of sunshine increase growth and numbers of phytoplankton.

All marine bryozoa are hermaphrodites and tend to start their life cycle as male and then later become female, though there are always a number that are simultaneously male and female, producing eggs and sperm at the same time. After sexual reproduction bryozoa have a larval stage that swims around before settling down to develop. It then undergoes a metamorphosis during the course of which its entire internal structure is rebuilt.

They are eaten by fish, sea slugs, sea urchins, sea spiders, crustaceans, starfish and mites. Bryozoa can become a serious threat to kelp and can carry disease into fish farms. Moreover they have posed a serious threat to pipelines and ships' hulls by excessive growth.

CARTILAGINOUS FISH

Chondrichthyes or cartilaginous fish first appeared in the oceans about 450 million years ago – before the time of the dinosaurs – and are generally considered more primitive than almost any species on the planet. They are divided into two subclasses depending primarily on the arrangement and number of their gill slits.

Sharks, rays and skates are part of one class known as Elasmobranchii. They are distinguished by a minimum of five gill slits on each side, one spiracle – or circular slit – behind each eye, dermal teeth across the skin of the upper body surface, an upper jaw that is largely detached from the skull and a lower tooth jaw.

The second, much smaller class consists of more primeval, deep ocean fish that are distinguished by having a single gill opening on each side, tooth plates and a skull with an attached upper jaw. The proper name is Holocephali (aka the chimaeras or ghost sharks).

Sharks are perhaps the most feared and effective killer in the oceans, most notably the great white shark (*Carcharodon carcharias*) and the hammerhead shark (*Sphyrnidae* spp.) which are described as 'apex predators', in other words at the top of the food chain with nothing but man to fear. Many are scavengers living off other sea dwellers and even waste thrown from ships. Between them they can eat everything from zooplankton to shellfish, fish, turtles, birds, seals and even whales.

▲ *This close-up of a great white shark clearly demonstrates the distinctive characteristics of the Elasmobranchii classification.*

Some sharks are more closely related to rays than they are to other sharks, having evolved into a wide range of shapes and sizes that are all highly specialized for a particular habitat or diet. The smallest cartilaginous fish is the cookiecutter shark (*Isistius brasiliensis*), which measures less than 50 cm (20 in) long, as opposed to its cousin the whale shark (*Rhincodon typhus*), which grows to 15 m (49 ft) and is the largest fish in the oceans.

Most cartilaginous fish must stay swimming to keep oxygenated water moving through their gills, even while sleeping. If they don't they will sink to the ocean floor and die. This is because they do not have swim bladders for buoyancy. It is a slightly different story for sharks which can float thanks to a large oil-filled liver which makes up 30 per cent of their body mass.

Built without bone, cartilaginous fish have skeletons made of cartilage, which has half the density of bone and considerably more flexibility and durability. However, most have some bone-

▲ *Perhaps the most feared killer in the oceans, this great white shark leaps above the surface of the water.*

like calcified cartilage in their teeth and sometimes in their vertebrae.

All species have two pairs of fins; one supported by the pectoral girdle and the other by the pelvic girdle. In addition, they have either one or two dorsal fins, ventral fins supported by girdles of the internal skeleton, a caudal fin and an anal fin. Both sharks and rays breathe through gill openings and are powered partially by their tails, in which the vertebral column extends into the larger top lobe. This is properly known as a heterocercal tail.

These creatures all lack ribs to support the inner organs, which means that, once out of water in a fishing boat's net, say, the larger specimens are crushed by their own body weight before they have time to suffocate.

Both sharks and rays have tough skin composed of tiny dermal teeth, scientifically called placoid scales, giving the skin a very rough, sandpapery texture. Indeed, it was once used as sandpaper. All the scales are oriented in the same direction from snout to tail, and protect and streamline the fish as well as helping to prevent parasites from establishing a hold. The tip of each tooth is composed of dentine overlaid by a layer of dental enamel, and the base is made from bone that anchors it to the skin. The size, shape and placement of these teeth vary

◀ *The shape of the hammerhead shark's head is believed to have evolved to enhance the animal's vision.*

from species to species, for instance a ray has clear skin without dermal teeth but, instead, on the upper tail surface and on its back, the teeth have grown into large, strong, deadly spines.

Sharks and rays have jaw teeth that are modified dermal teeth. As they wear down they fall out and are replaced by new teeth from behind. These new teeth line up in rows ready to replace their predecessors. Most large sharks have two or three layers of teeth but mature great white sharks can have up to five rows of teeth. It's thought that a large shark can lose up to 30,000 teeth or more across its lifespan. Most teeth are replaced one at a time as required at a rate of once every ten days to eight weeks. This can happen because the teeth are embedded into the shark's gum instead of being fixed into the jaw bone, which is more usual among fish. The shape and size of the teeth depends on the shark species and its diet: big predators need large, triangular, serrated, sharp teeth, fish eaters have needle-like spines while others have developed flattened teeth for crushing crustaceans and mollusks.

All cartilaginous fish use internal fertilization and the male's primary sexual organ is located at the inner rear end of the pectoral (pelvic) fin. There are three principle methods of reproduction. The commonest is called ovoviviparous, when eggs are laid and hatched within the female. The young then continue to grow within the mother, feeding off the remnants of egg yolk before being passed out of her body. She will choose to do this in a sheltered area well away from predators but where there is plenty of food for the young shark. Popular locations are shallow reefs, bays and the mouths of rivers. It's important the new born shark is fully functional and able to fend for itself from the moment it leaves its mother's body as she disappears immediately after giving birth. The advantage of this method of reproduction is that the young are less vulnerable to predators as they are already relatively large by the time they are born. Various types of dogfish have the longest gestation period which can last anything up to two years.

The second method is to produce eggs. These are known as oviparous species and include sea-bed dwelling rays, chimaeras and sharks. Females produce

▲ *Few marine creatures are safe from the predatory dangers of sharks; here bronze whaler sharks enjoy an offshore feeding frenzy.*

a leathery purse-like case that attaches itself by means of twisted tendrils to seaweed, rocks or the sea bed. They are often referred to as 'mermaid's purses' and empty ones are found washed up on beaches from time to time. Some Chondrichthyes will guard their eggs, but most just swim off.

A few rare species are viviparous and develop their offspring in utero fed by a placenta-type arrangement very similar to mammals, so the young are born fully developed. Species using this method include the hammerheads and the smoothhounds (*Mustelus* spp.).

▶ *A newborn swell shark hatches from its egg case to face the perils of ocean life.*

Sharks

Few creatures are feared like sharks. But to imagine that swimmers and surfers are at perpetual risk from a voracious predator is a shocking falsehood. Fatal shark attacks barely reach double figures in any 12 month period. One estimate says the chances of being killed in a shark attack amount to about one per cent of the risk of being struck by lightning. Meanwhile some 100 million sharks perish at the hands of man in the same period.

A shark rarely attacks a human because it is hungry. The most likely reason for a brush with sharks is because they are both curious and clumsy.

There is very little that is uniform about the 440 species of shark in the oceans of the world. Some are greatly endangered and few in number, others are abundant and thriving. Sharks are common in waters down to depths of 2,000 m (6,562 ft) and less often found at depths of 3,000 m (9,843 ft). The smallest species is the dwarf lanternshark (*Etmopterus perryi*), a type of dogfish found off the north coast of South America,

at around 21 cm (8 in) and the largest is the whale shark that swims warm tropical seas and grows to about 12 m (39 ft). Most species live for about 30 years, although the whale shark is thought to live for over a hundred years. Only a few species live solitary lives and even they gather together for breeding and hunting purposes; many shark species are social animals and congregate in large numbers.

Sharks breathe through either five or seven gills located in rows behind their head. Normally a shark takes in water through its mouth and oxygen is extracted from it by the gills. The water is then passed out through the gill slits in a process known as ram ventilation. Even at rest most sharks have to pump water over their gills to keep the constant supply of oxygenated water running through their system.

Additionally, the spiracle behind the animal's eye helps bottom-dwelling sharks breathe when resting on the sea bed. It means they can take in water when the gills are obscured by the

▼ *A multitude of fish take cover underneath the bulk of a whale shark.*

sands of the sea floor, pump it through the gill chamber and then release it through the gill slits without taking aboard huge amounts of mud or debris. Some of the larger, active Chondrichthyes have no need for spiracles and either have one that's severely reduced or none at all.

Scientists are no longer convinced by the terms warm- and cold-blooded as the definitions are deemed too narrow. Sharks are perhaps a prime example of why. Most sharks are cold-blooded or poikilothermic, so their internal body temperature is the same as the surrounding water. A few, such as the shortfin mako shark (*Isurus oxyrinchus*), are warm blooded or homeothermic and, through a combination of muscles and blood, generate their own body heat. The shortfin is also the fastest shark, capable of bursts of speed of up to 50 kph (31 mph) and it is thought the two things may be related. Otherwise most sharks swim at an average of 8 kph (5 mph) which they increase to around 19 kph (12 mph) when hunting and attacking. The caudal fin provides the forward thrust, the dorsal fin gives balance and the pectoral fin acts as a rudder and provides upward force.

Almost all sharks are carnivorous, but each eats a specialized diet and uses particular hunting methods that vary according to species. Some species such as tiger sharks (*Galeocerdo cuvier*) are voracious and will eat almost anything they can catch.

▲ *The basking shark is a passive filter feeder, filtering zooplankton, small fish and invertebrates at or close to the surface with their mouths wide open and gill rakers erect.*

Basking sharks (*Cetorhinus maximus*), whale sharks and the extremely rare megamouth shark (*Megachasma pelagios*) are all filter feeders and live off plankton and small fish. Consequently they have small, insignificant teeth because these are not needed for feeding.

Ocean-bed living sharks tend to live on a diet of crustaceans that they crush and grind with flat teeth. Cookiecutter sharks are scavengers, living off the scraps left by others, tearing and ripping at the flesh of already dead prey.

Sharks with numerous, large, sharp teeth swallow their prey whole or tear off chunks, then swallow the mouthful unchewed, which is what the notorious great white shark does.

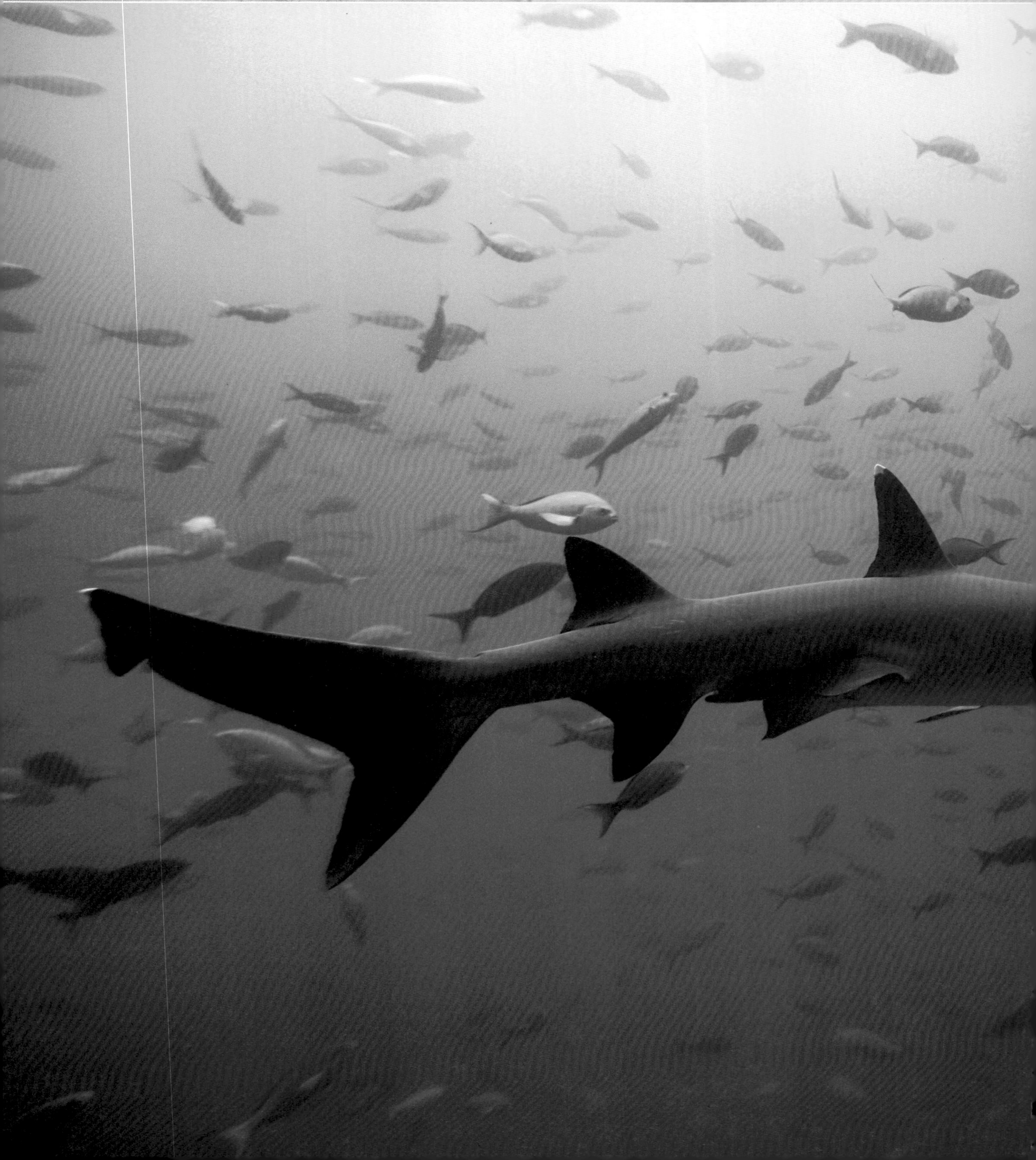

◀ *Whitetip reef sharks hunt primarily at night, when many fish are asleep and easily taken.*

▶ *The angel shark is a benthic creature whose coloration matches the sandy bottom where it waits to ambush its prey*

Some species, such as the viper dogfish (*Trigonognathus kabeyai*), have outward thrusting teeth with which they strike their prey, impale them and then swallow them whole. Thresher sharks (*Alopias vulpinus*) are so-named for the way they use their long and lethal tails to stir up the water and stun their prey. Many species, typically the migratory ones such as the small whitetip reef shark (*Triaenodon obesus*), cooperate to hunt in packs and track down their prey before going in for the kill and communal feeding.

Some species of sea-bed dwelling sharks such as angel sharks (*Squatina* spp.) ambush predators and are camouflaged to match their surroundings so they can catch unsuspecting passing fish.

If they eat something overly large or toxic, most sharks have the ability to vomit unwanted matter and even to turn their stomachs inside out to expel food.

Sharks have the greatest electrical sensitivity of any animal and can detect the electromagnetic fields that all living things give off. With hundreds or even thousands of electroreceptors (called ampullae of Lorenzini) they can find prey even when it is hidden under a layer of sand. It is thought sharks use the Earth's magnetic field for orientation and navigation.

They have other tools in their armory as well. Although sharks generally have good hearing with which they locate prey, they often find food through their remarkable sense of smell. They can detect blood in the water at one part per million. They also sense the chemicals found in the guts of many species and use that to locate them. It is not known how well sharks can see – it probably varies considerably between species – but they can contract and dilate their pupils according to light levels and are thought to see comparatively well in the ocean depths. Some species such as the great white shark roll their eyes backwards into their sockets to protect them when they strike their prey, which implies that in evolutionary terms their eyes are important if not essential.

Most sharks take a long time to become sexually mature so where population numbers are low, it can take years for the species to recover. Their numbers are threatened by commercial shark fishing which is responsible for their decline – over 100 of the 400 or so shark species are commercially fished, endangering the continued existence of many. Other factors related to shark decline include loss of habitat, pollution and coastal development. Some of the most at risk species include the bluegray carpetshark (*Heteroscyllium colcloughi*), the deepwater spiny dogfish (*Centrophorus squamosus*), the flapnose houndshark (*Scylliogaleus quecketti*) and the great white shark.

▲ *Sicklefin mobulas glide gracefully through the Atlantic Ocean.*

▼ *A close-up of the underside of a blackspotted stingray.*

Rays and stingrays

Rays have distinctive broad, flat, rhomboid-shaped bodies with eyes and spiracles located on the dark upper surface and mouth and gills on the lower pale underside.

Also known as batoids, they belong to the superorder Batoidea which contains 13 families and over 500 species. Almost all are found in tropical, warm and temperate coastal waters but a few deep ocean species live at depths of 3,000 m (9,843 ft).

Most rays have five gill slits (although one family, the Hexatrygonidae, has six) on their underside under the pectoral fins. They lack an anal fin but have a clearly defined slender tail. Most have two dorsal fins and many species appear to have developed broad wings but these are in fact evolved pectoral fins.

Rays are camouflaged by countershading, meaning the upper parts are darker than the lower, which hides them from predators looking down at the ocean bed. When seen from beneath the ray is almost invisible against the light coming through the surface of the water. The great white shark also uses countershading to stalk its prey.

Using well-developed spiracles instead of their mouths to take water aboard, the rays pass it out through their gills. They exist on a diet of ocean-floor dwelling fish, mollusks, crustaceans and oysters for which they have evolved rounded shell-crushing teeth. All batoids are viviparous with the exception of skates, which are oviparous, depositing their fertilized eggs in a rectangular horn-like case on the ocean bed.

Rays swim with a unique vertical undulating wave motion from front to rear because their large flat bodies are fused with their pectoral fins. It is known as rajiform swimming. The huge manta ray (*Manta birostris*) is one of the few batoids to live in the open seas, often near coral reefs, and it is also one of the minority that filter-feeds off plankton. One of the biggest and most interesting marine animals, it is only found in tropical and sub-tropical waters although it will migrate long distances, probably in its perpetual search for food. These rays can grow up to 7.6 m (25 ft) long, over 6 m (20 ft) across, weigh 2,268 kg (5,000 lb) and live for an average 20 years. They also have the largest brain-to-body ratio of all the cartilaginous fish and, unlike other rays, have their mouth on their upper surface. The manta ray can move very fast through the water, like a bird flapping its wings. For reasons unknown there are many more male manta rays than female, so the males have to search hard to find a mate. When they do they often have to fight for her. Sharks and orcas are their main predators.

Stingrays, which are common in coastal tropical and sub-tropical waters, are distinguished from other rays by their lethal stinger. It is a modified dermal denticle or tooth of skin only used for

▶ *Three blotched fantail stingrays swim over the Ellaidhoo House Reef in the Maldives.*

▲ *A manta ray feeds on plankton and fish larvae, filtered from the water passing through its gills as it swims.*

self-defense. The venom is stored in glands on its underside. Lurking under a layer of sand, stingrays habitually wait for prey rather than hunt for it. They cannot see their target and instead rely on an acute sense of smell and their electroreceptors (the same ampullae of Lorenzo used by sharks). They eat small fish as well as crustaceans and molluscs. Stingrays are ovoviviparous producing up to 13 live young at a time.

Holocephali

The Holocephali were once an extensive group of cartilaginous fish but the majority have long since disappeared and are now only known through the fossil record. Only one order, the Chimaeriformes, survive; popularly called chimaeras they are known as ghost sharks, ratfish or even rabbitfish and comprise three families of about 40 species. Although they share some of the physical characteristics of bony fish their closest living relatives are the sharks, despite the fact that their evolutionary tree split almost 400 million years ago.

Chimaera inhabit all the oceans of the world and are strange looking creatures of the deep oceans living along the soft, muddy bottoms of the deeper continental shelves. Relatively little is known about them as they rarely swim above 200 m (656 ft). The only exceptions are the rabbit fish (*Signanus* spp.) and spotted ratfish (*Hydrolagus colliei*) which occasionally venture nearer the surface of Puget Sound and British Columbia foraging for food in the mud and sand during the hours of darkness. However, recent studies of the deep are discovering new species.

Chimaera have a cartilaginous skeleton covered by an elongated body covered with a smooth skin of placoid scales. They have a big head with large eyes and often a modified snout that acts as a sensory organ. Breathing is carried out through a single gill opening that, unlike those of sharks, is covered with a flap called an operculum. These creatures are generally smaller than sharks, only growing to a maximum 150 cm (4.9 ft) long. Their upper jaw is fused to the skull and their mouth contains three pairs of sharp-edged grinding tooth plates; two pairs in the upper jaw and one in the lower jaw. They use these to feed mainly on shellfish and bottom-living invertebrates.

Lacking the grace of some sea life, Chimaeras swim by beating their broad pectoral fins simultaneously to go forward or alternately to change direction, while lashing their whip-like tail from side to side. Many species have a venomous spine located on the leading edge of the dorsal fin that they raise in time of danger, but otherwise it lies flat and unnoticed against the body.

▲ *The elephant fish is a primitive fish, relative to sharks, that lives in the deep sea and uses its trunk-like snout to detect prey on the sea bottom.*

▶ *The spotted ratfish gets its characteristic name from a pointed rat-like tail.*

Another unusual feature in many species is that the males have retractable sexual appendages in front of the pelvic fins (like sharks) as well as a tiny barbed appendage on their forehead for clasping their mate. Chimaera are oviparous and females lay their eggs in two spiral-shaped leather pouches which they deposit on the sea bed. After six months to a year, the young hatch and immediately disappear into the ocean depths.

CNIDARIANS

After sharks, jellyfish are probably the most feared of the ocean's species. So it is a surprise to learn that these creatures are closely related to corals and sea anemones, among the least threatening of the sea's inhabitants.

They are all members of the Cnidaria class, which has two sub-phyla: the Anthozoa and the Medusozoa. The former is made up of the corals and sea anemones, and the latter the box jellyfish, sea wasps, hydroids and jellyfish. There are more than 9,000 different Cnidarian species.

Sea anemones and sea pens

Sea anemones and sea pens both look like plants yet they can if necessary detach themselves from their anchored bases and move to another position. They all have specialized stinging cells called nematocysts, with which they capture various prey. Although they can move, sea anemones are unable to chase down their food so they have to sit and wait for it to come into range. However, the nematocysts located on the ends of their tentacles give them some scope when it comes to hunting.

When prey comes sufficiently close, it will be quickly enveloped by the tentacles and then passed into the mouth. Some species have no more than a score of tentacles while others have hundreds at their disposal. The poisons contained in them are neurotoxic and usually paralyze the victim quickly. This allows the stationary sea anemone to overcome animals that are relatively large in comparison, such as prawns and small fish. Sea anemones also sieve small particles from the surrounding water for consumption. Sea pens use their stinging cells in a similar manner, but tend to feed on much smaller, planktonic creatures.

There are many different species of sea anemone – they are divided into 46 families, and within them there is a considerable range of sizes. The smallest are only a few millimeters across, but the largest – Mertens' sea anemone (*Stichodactyla mertensii*), can grow to more than 1m (3 ft 3 in) in diameter. Most attach themselves to a suitable rock with an adhesive pedal disc. A few are free-ranging, floating upside down at the top of the ocean with help from a gas chamber in the pedal disk.

Sea anemones all have a cylindrical body with a single internal cavity where the major metabolic functions are performed. This includes such activities as digestion, respiration and circulation. The tentacles pass food into this via a single opening, and any waste products are later ejected from it. Many sea anemones form symbiotic relationships with various species of algae. In return for nourishment and protection, these simple photosynthetic plants produce oxygen for their hosts.

▶ *While a few species of sea anemone are pelagic – having a gas chamber within the pedal disc that allows them to float upside down in the water – these yellow cluster anemones are attached to the sea bed.*

Sea pens (Pennatulacea), which are exclusively marine, are found across the temperate and tropical parts of the world. Although some species live in shallow waters only 10 m (33 ft.) or so below the surface, many live at depths in excess of 2,000 m (6,562 ft) where there's less turbulence. They are often brightly colored, can grow to heights of around 2 m (6ft 7 in), and possess large numbers of polyps along the leaf-like 'fronds', each of which has eight tentacles. They are preyed upon by many animals, including nudibranchs and starfish, but have two primary forms of defense. Firstly they can eject water at an encroaching enemy and withdraw tightly into their stalk. Also, they have bioluminescence to deter hungry predators. It is thought that sea pens live for about 100 years.

Jellyfish

Jellyfish were among the first multicellular animals to evolve.
Remarkably, given jellyfish texture, the first fossils date from
several hundred million years ago. They were so successful that
jellyfish quickly established an ecological niche for themselves
and have hardly changed since. Somewhat surprisingly,
there are relatively few species, with only 200 or so being
recognized by science. They make up for the lack of diversity
with numbers, however, being one of the most common sea
creatures in the world. As they are not fish, or even like fish,
some people prefer to call them jellies or sea jellies.

Most of a jellyfish's body is water, with much of the rest
being made up of a special jelly that is held between two
membranous layers. In effect that means many are virtually
transparent in the water. Rather than a nervous system they
have a nerve net in their outer layer that responds to the
presence of other sea creatures.

▲ *The largest known jellyfish is the lion's
mane jellyfish which has been recorded
at a diameter of 2.3 m (7 ft 6 in) and
with tentacles 36.5 m (120 ft) long.*

Mobility can be a problem. Some species lack any significant
muscles and accordingly they are unable to control where
they travel. This means they are completely tied to the whim of
wind and tide and end up drifting wherever nature's elements
take them. Others pulsate rather than swim, giving them
limited independent direction.

The smallest jellyfish measures less than a centimeter in length
and the largest has a tentacle spread of over 36 m (118 ft
11ins) and a body more than 2 m (6 ft 6 ins) in diameter.

Typically a jellyfish diet consists of small fish, crustaceans and
plankton caught using long tentacles which are equipped with
large numbers of stinging cells. When prey has been secured,
the tentacles are raised towards the mouth and the hapless

victims are slowly consumed. Some species have toxins that are powerful enough to kill or seriously injure humans. Lacking a proper digestive system a jellyfish digests using the special lining of its gastrovascular cavity, the equivalent of a stomach.

Box jellyfish

Box jellyfish (Cubozoa) are distinct from true jellyfish as their umbrellas bear a number of structural differences. For a start they are, as the name would suggest, box-shaped. They also have a special kind of one-way valve which is located underneath the cubic umbrella. This is called a velarium and its purpose is to increase the creature's power and speed. They also have other important features, like true eyes and a more complex nervous system.

Infamously, their stings contain some of the most toxic venom known in the animal kingdom. The venom is delivered by vast numbers of small stinging cells shaped like harpoons and called cnidocytes. Typically, there are around half a million of these per tentacle, and they are used for killing prey as well as forming a very efficient defense mechanism against potential predators. The highest numbers of human deaths caused by box jellyfish stings occur in Australia, Indonesia and Malaysia, with children being considered more vulnerable than adults. However, it is only a few species that are lethal to humans and many people survive an encounter with a box jellyfish, escaping with nothing more traumatic than a rash.

Box jellyfish can be found in most of the world's tropical and sub-tropical seas, including the Pacific, Indo-Pacific, Indian and Atlantic Oceans, as well as the Mediterranean Sea. They range from Japan and California in the north, to South Africa and New Zealand in the south.

▶ *A box jellyfish pulls its prey, in this case, a stung shrimp, towards its mouth.*

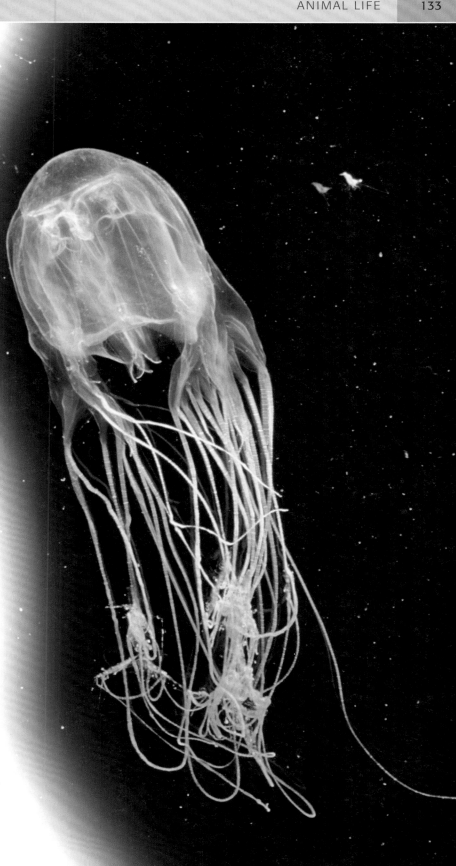

ECHINODERMS

Echinoderms are a large, varied and long established group, with about 7,000 species in total. Best known among its family members are the starfish or sea stars (Asteroidea), sea urchins (Echinoidea), crinoids or feather-stars (Crinoidea), sea cucumbers (Holothuroidea) and brittle stars (Ophiuroidea). Knowledge of their ancestry is especially good as their hard skeletons fossilize well, giving science an excellent paleontological record.

From this, it has been determined that many other types of echinoderm also evolved, but that these did not thrive, eventually dying out altogether. Perhaps as many as 13,000 in total fall into this category. The entire phylum or grouping is exclusively marine, with representatives being found in all the world's seas and oceans from the shallowest pools to the abyssal depths. It is the largest phylum to have no representatives living on land or in fresh water.

The members of this group all have bodies which are radially symmetrical and only possess very basic nervous systems, lacking distinct brains. This has its advantages, however, as if they are cut into pieces, they are able to regenerate themselves. In the right circumstances a severed starfish leg, for example, will grow into a fully functioning individual.

There are separate sexes and, at the appropriate time, the males release clouds of sperm into the water while the females eject their eggs in vast numbers. Beyond that process, fertilization is left to chance. Sperm and egg drift freely on the tide, in the hope rather than the expectation of a happy union. Although this is a seemingly haphazard method, the odds are vastly improved due to the sheer numbers of eggs and sperm released.

Where fertilization is successful, the eggs develop for a time then hatch into free-swimming larvae. These have bilaterally symmetrical bodies, but as they mature they acquire the radial form of the adults. As there are so many predators that specialize in sieving small creatures like these from the oceans' waters for food, the mortality rate of young echinoderms is very high and few survive to adulthood.

The group varies tremendously both in size and form. Sea cucumbers, for instance, have mouths located at the front of their bodies, but others, like the starfish and sea urchins, have their mouths positioned underneath. The smallest starfish are only a few millimeters across, but the largest crinoids may grow to over a meter in height.

▶ *Three members of the Echinoderm family in close proximity: a sea star, california sea cucumber and red sea urchin.*

Starfish

Starfish, which are also known as seas stars in some parts of the world, usually have a body with five radial arms. Some close cousins, however, can have as many as 14 arms – this is especially so with sun stars. These arms are not used as their main means of locomotion though – this is the job of the hundreds of small tubular feet which are arranged across most of their lower surfaces. The feet are operated by hydraulic pressure and can be used for both movement and tackling prey. In total there are about 1,800 different species of starfish. They are distributed throughout the world's seas and oceans, from the shallows of coral reefs and tidal rock pools to the very deepest reaches.

Different species of starfish feed on different things. While many eat coral polyps, most subsist on decaying plant or animal matter. Almost all of them are also rampant opportunists and will attack and consume more or less any creature that they can find and overcome. In such circumstances, their tubular feet can be used to defeat some unlikely prey. When attacking a well-defended bivalve such as a mussel or a clam, for instance, the starfish will wrap itself around the victim and use hydraulic power to prize the two halves of the shell open. The fleshy contents are then consumed at leisure.

Brittle stars

Although brittle stars look very similar to starfish, with their long, thin, flexible arms, they are members of a completely different class of echinoderms. The majority inhabit deep water environments, where they feed by a number of different means. Some survive by filtering edible particles and small organisms from the surrounding water. Others are specialists in scavenging from the decaying remains of animals and plants that have fallen from the waters above. A significant number are hunters of small creatures such as shrimps or marine worms.

The species of brittle stars that live in shallow water typically hide during the day in such places as narrow crevices or under rocks. They then emerge at night to feed when there is less risk of being discovered by predators like seagulls and skuas. Unlike starfish, which move around on their tubular feet, brittle stars actually use their arms as their main means of locomotion. When they find something edible, the tube feet are used to pick it up. Little by little, the item is passed along and gradually moved towards the mouth, where it is ingested. They are distributed throughout the world's seas and oceans, and vary in size from small species of only a few millimeters right up to the largest examples which may reach as much as 60 cm (2 ft) in diameter.

◄ *A Suenson's brittle star on an azure vase sponge on the sea bed off Honduras.*

▼ *The predatory crown of thorns starfish feeds on the polyps of a stony coral in the Indian Ocean.*

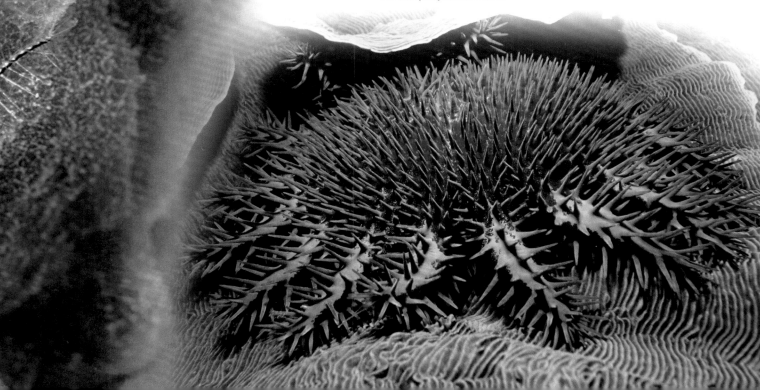

▲ *Sea urchins, such as this Slate pencil urchin, are sensitive to touch, light and chemicals.*

Sea urchins

Closely related to starfish and brittle stars, sea urchins have a hard globular shell which is known as a 'test' in place of arm-like structures. This leaves them unable to hide in tightly-confined spaces and they are therefore open to attack by predators. In order to defend themselves, they have evolved a covering of very sharp spines. In many species these are further re-enforced with venomous chemicals. This provides a very effective means of protection. Proof that it works, if any were needed, comes from the fact that they have changed little in tens of millions of years.

Yet in spite of this they are still preyed upon by a wide variety of creatures including crabs, fish, wolf eels, sea otters, some starfish and mollusks, birds, and humans. As they are incapable of moving quickly, their omnivorous diet is restricted to fixed or slow-moving animals and plants, such as seaweed, algae, sponges, barnacles and mollusks. They will also scavenge any dead material that they can find.

Sea urchins are found throughout the world's seas and oceans at all its many levels. The class contains around 700 different species, the largest of which is the red sea urchin (*Strongylocentrotus franciscanus*). This can grow to a size of nearly 20 cm (8 in) in diameter, and is found in the Pacific Ocean. Others have smaller shells but make up for this by possessing much longer spines.

Sea Cucumbers

Structurally, sea cucumbers are quite unlike other members of the echinoderm phylum. More caterpillar than cucumber, they have a series of tentacles – as many as thirty – arranged around their mouths. These are used to crumble food, which is typically detritus on the sea bed, which they eat as well as whatever floating plankton is in the vicinity. Like other members of the group they move around using small tube feet that are hydraulically powered. They live in or on the ocean floor, with many species constructing special burrows by digging into the sea bed to give themselves a degree of protection from predators. Many live in herds. Although some have evolved to retain toxic chemicals, they are still preyed upon by all manner of animals including turtles, crabs, fish and humans. Threatened sea cucumbers throw up sticky threads in an effort of trap or hinder any predator. Reproduction between species varies but some keep their young in a pouch until they are sufficiently mature to survive the perils of the ocean. The largest species of sea cucumber is the tiger's tail (*Holothuria thomasi*), which can reach lengths of around 2 m (6 ft 6 in) but most of the others are considerably smaller. In China, where sea cucumbers are widely eaten, they are farmed.

Feather-stars

Among the most curious of all creatures, feather-stars look like flowers. Consequently they are known as sea lilies or – more technically – crinoids. They have changed little since they first evolved during the Ordovician Period, around 450 million years ago, and there are plenty in fossil form. While they live in all marine environments they are most commonly found in deeper water. About 600 species are currently known to science. Although they bear many similarities to plants, having a main stem off which a number of smaller branches grow, they are actually animals. One of the more obvious

◄ *A colony of feather stars adorn this coral reef and work in partnership with its neighbor.*

▲ *A sea apple sea cucumber with its tentacles extended for feeding.*

distinctions is that they are able to detach themselves from the sea bed and move, either by crawling or swimming, to a new site whenever necessary. The most common reason for doing so is a shortage of food. They eat minute planktonic creatures which are filtered from the surrounding water. But they have also been observed moving away from predators, most notably the sea urchin.

▼ *The lamprey when in parasite phase feeds on fish by rasping through their skin.*

JAWLESS FISH

Jawless fish are so primitive that scientists do not consider them to be fish at all but a creature from an earlier evolutionary stage. It seems they are the ancestor of today's fish and reptiles – and ultimately of mankind.

The vast majority of jawless fish, which are classified as Agnatha, are now extinct. All that remains are hagfish and lampreys, which can be termed living fossils as they are remarkably similar to fossilized remains dating back 360 million years.

Although they share a number of characteristics, hagfish and lampreys are in different groupings. However, both have mouths with no bony support or cartilage, they lack limbs or paired fins and have a cartilaginous endoskeleton that supports their elongated, scaleless body. They have seven or more paired gill pouches and a caudal fin and tail. Internally they lack an identifiable stomach possessing instead an extended gut. They die if removed from the water. All are cold-blooded and, when living in cold water, slow their metabolism at which time they require little food. Most are also hermaphrodite and lay eggs. In appearance both could be mistaken for eels.

All Agnatha possess a notochord, a very primitive form of rod-shaped, flexible backbone. This is present in their larvae and persists into the adult; also their skull remains cartilaginous throughout their lives.

Lampreys

Lampreys live in most cold and temperate coastal waters around the world. Adults can grow up to 100 cm (3 ft 3 in) long, with large eyes, a nostril on the top of the head and seven gills on each flank. They are parasitic and attach to other creatures with their funnel-like mouth via sharp teeth that they use to pierce the skins of their fish victims. Some thrive on blood while for others the favored food is muscle.

Gender neutral lampreys are ultimately doomed. They reproduce only once and after laying eggs the relevant orifice remains open allowing a fungus to enter and infest their intestines. After burying their eggs in fresh water riverbeds they return to the sea to die. When the larvae hatch they swim out to sea but remain larval for four years.

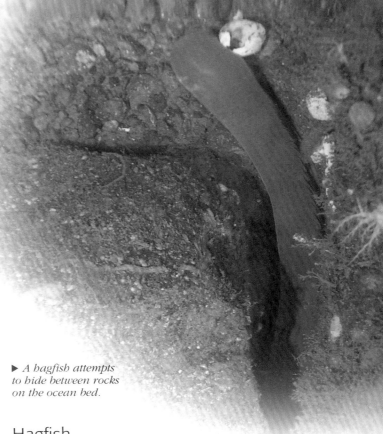

▶ *A hagfish attempts to hide between rocks on the ocean bed.*

Hagfish

There are 60 species of hagfish, many of them living in numbers together on the sea bed where they have changed little over the last 300 million years.

Hagfish grow to an average 50 cm (1 ft 8 in) long although some species are considerably longer. They have flexible, finless, elongated bodies that contain two brains, four hearts and a paddle-shaped tail. Hagfish are unique in having a skull but no backbone which is why they are sometimes put into a different animal classification. They have simple eyes, a single nostril and six or eight barbels around a mouth that contains comb-shaped teeth set into two retractable horny jaw plates. Their primary defense mechanism lies in their skin, which contains numerous glands that secrete a copious quantity of slime which inflates into a gelatinous, sticky mess on contact with water.

Little is known about hagfish reproduction but they are thought to be hermaphrodite. Different species lay anything from one to 30 eggs that gestate and hatch young fully-formed young.

Hagfish feed on dead, rotting or dying marine animals by ripping into the body cavity and eating from the inside out. Their slow metabolism means they can survive for months between feeds.

MARINE MAMMALS

Marine mammals share the same two basic characteristics as their terrestrial cousins – they need air to breathe and give birth to live young which they then suckle with high-fat content milk (up to 50 per cent). However only a very small percentage of the Earth's mammals live in and around the oceans and even then only two orders of mammals are entirely ocean-living – the Cetacea and the Sirenia.

There are 120 species of marine mammal, all of them descended from terrestrial ancestors and all evolved for life at sea through modified appendages, adapted body temperature controls and streamlined or 'hydrodynamic' body shapes. Because of their terrestrial roots, the spine of marine mammals articulates with an up-and-down movement – unlike a fish's spine which moves from side to side. This is why most mammals have horizontal fins and tails and most fish vertical fins and tails.

Marine mammals have a thick, insulating layer of blubber with which they protect internal organs from the cold and prevent general heat loss. This way they maintain a much higher internal body temperature than other marine life forms. The group includes 4 species of sirenian (the dugong and manatees), about 85 species of cetacean (whales, dolphins and porpoises) and around 23 species of marine carnivore (the walrus, sea lion, various seals and the sea otter), which are partially land-dwelling.

▶ *This rearview image of a humpback whale clearly illustrates the fin and tail differences between marine mammals and fish.*

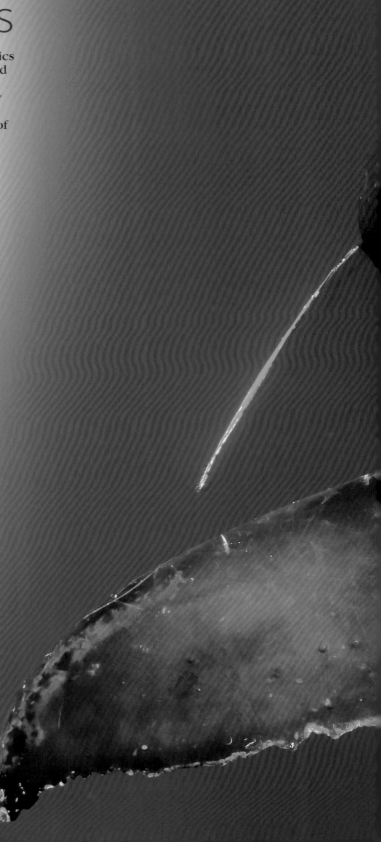

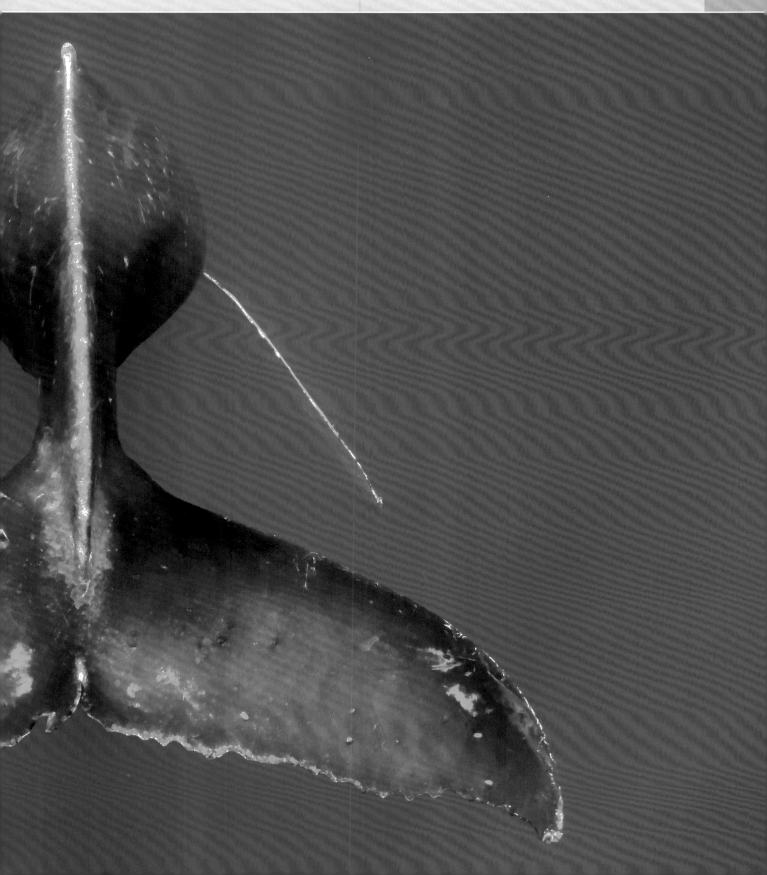

Bright spark of the sea

Cetaceans are among the most intelligent (and best-loved) of all marine creatures. There are around 85 cetacean species, sub-divided into two groups, and all, except five types of freshwater dolphin, live in the ocean. The name cetacean comes from the Greek for 'sea monster' (*ketos*) and Latin for 'large sea animal' (*cetus*). Not surprising, perhaps, that their closest terrestrial relative is the hippopotamus.

In classifying this group of mammals scientists have divided them into two suborders, the Mysticeti and the Odontoceti. The former comprises the 13 species of baleen whale while the latter is made up of some 73 species of toothed whale including narwhal, sperm, beluga and killer whales, as well as several species of porpoise and dolphin. But all cetaceans are really just different types of whale. Dolphins may look different with their distinctive beak and a mouth full of conical teeth, and similarly porpoises with their blunt noses and spade-shaped, flat teeth. Yet like whales these animals have little or no body hair, sometimes just a few bristles around the head area.

Size is obviously a distinguishing factor and some members of the family are truly leviathans of the sea. In fact, the largest mammal ever discovered was a 33 m (108 ft) long blue whale weighing a hefty 135 tonnes (149 tons). Quite apart from its other ocean-friendly adaptations, such a gigantic creature could never live on land as it would effectively be crushed by its own weight.

About 50 million years ago cetaceans completed their transformation from land mammals while retaining their favored biological traits – oxygen-breathing lungs, warm blood and the advantages of giving live birth – an improvement in infant mortality rates. They also continued to suckle their young for as long as required, an important factor in survival rates.

In their adopted environment they benefitted hugely from their streamlined, almost hairless, bodies which produced only minimal friction in the water. Their one-time front limbs were now fins or flippers while former rear limbs became little more than an echo from the past, an evolutionary throwback no longer even attached to the backbone. The reason why these limbs became surplus to requirements is clear once you appreciate the cetacean development of a powerful, elongated tail. This tail, terminating in the familiar two horizontally-flattened divisions known as 'flukes', achieves immense thrust as it is thrashed up and down.

A cetacean's skull is streamlined and contains a (usually) large brain, small eyes on either side of the head and ears with no obvious external parts (a tiny hole behind the eye is the only indication). All beaked cetaceans such as dolphins and porpoises have binocular vision forwards and downwards in contrast to blunt-nosed cetaceans such as sperm whales, which have comparatively good vision either side but cannot see directly ahead. Curiously, the eyes are sometimes marked by dark stains down the cheeks, giving the appearance of crying; in fact this is a greasy secretion which protects the eyes from saline water. In fact cetaceans don't have particularly good eyesight even though their eyes are adapted to collect as much light as possible when swimming at depth. They lean far more heavily on their hearing for navigation and decision-making.

These mammals don't possess any vocal chords although they do make constant communicating sounds – clicks, moans and whistles to the human ear – which they transmit through the skull and jaw bones. Most, but not all, cetaceans use sonar or echo location to build up a sound 'picture' of their surroundings (the only other mammals able to perform this handy feat are bats) and this allows them to hunt successfully even in the murkiest, darkest waters. Depending on the state and depth of the water they can hear over a distance of many kilometers and can locate noise sources with uncanny accuracy.

▶ *Three adult common bottlenose dolphins demonstrate their aerial ability off the coast of Honduras.*

◀ *Atlantic spotted dolphins hunting a school of snappers in the Caribbean.*

▲ *An orca pod surfaces in Alaska's Kenai Fjords National Park.*

The need for a hydrodynamic profile means there are no external reproductive organs. These are instead concealed within a thick layer of blubber, sandwiched between skin and flesh, which in some species can be over 30 cm (1 ft) thick. This ensures more than adequate protection for the reproductive system.

The nostril appears as either a single or double blowhole (also called a spout) on the top of the head. This is the main air intake – as with all other aquatic mammals cetaceans can drown if prevented from breathing air – and forms part of an ingenious breathing apparatus. The blowhole is covered with external flaps which close when the animal dives to prevent water entering the lungs. When it surfaces to breathe it blows a jet of water into the air, simultaneously exhaling warm, moisture-laden carbon dioxide. Each species of cetacean does this slightly differently, either in the shape of the venting jet, the angle it emerges or the height it reaches.

Of the two distinct sub-groups the Odontoceti, or toothed whales, bite and tear the flesh off their prey (typically seals, squids, fish and, occasionally, other weaker whales). But they don't chew their food, preferring to swallow it whole as soon as a digestible chunk comes off in their mouth. In contrast the Mysticeti (such as the minke, blue, and humpback whales) feed on plankton and krill filtered through a specialized structure called a baleen. This flattened modification of the mouth is composed of keratin – bundles of fibrous structural proteins which sieve out and trap nutrients.

Cetaceans are found in deep waters around the world as well as the shallower coastal fringes around continental shelves. Some are restless wanderers and still evade scientific understanding about their migration routes and breeding grounds. Many species will roam widely to find food, often searching for fish in the upwelling waters where the deep, protein-rich cold currents rise to the warmer surface. Whales are particularly fond of upwellings as hunting grounds.

Porpoises are known to swim vast distances and many migrate seasonally, spending the summer in the Arctic or Antarctic before returning to warmer latitudes once these waters start to freeze. In the milder habitat they give birth and seek to mate; a life cycle which has proved hugely successful. Like all cetaceans they face an increasing and unequal battle to survive human activity, particularly the factory fishing which sees so many 'accidentally' caught and killed in tuna nets. From a global perspective, though, it is whaling which still represents the greatest threat to species survival.

Whaling started to become an organized, international industry in the 17th century and since then whale numbers have been in decline – especially in the 20th century when factory ships slaughtered them by the thousand. By the mid-20th century many populations could not replenish themselves and global numbers fell into serious decline. It took many years before a public and scientific outcry against the industry forced politicians to act and it wasn't until 1986 that the International Whaling Commission declared that many species were in imminent danger of extinction and banned commercial whaling.

Since then the ban has been observed by every country except Norway, Iceland, Russia and Japan and populations have started to recover. But as females produce on average only one pup every other year it takes decades for a population to stabilize. Some species such as the blue whale (*Balaenoptera musculus*), the right whale (*Eubalaena* spp.) and the humpback whale (*Megaptera novaeangliae*) remain on the brink of extinction and may yet disappear despite international efforts.

▶ *An aerial view of dall's porpoise swimming in the calm water of Prince William Sound, Alaska.*

▼ *It is not yet known why whales, such as this humpback, breach themselves out of the water.*

Sirenians – a prehistoric legacy

Sirenians evolved over 50 million years ago and most are known only through the fossil record. However four species remain: the dugongs (Dugongidae) and three species of manatee (Trichechidae). Commonly called sea cows, the name of this scientific order derives from mariners' legends about mermaids – or 'sirens' – for which they were supposedly mistaken. They are thought to have evolved from a wading, plant-eating mammal of which the elephant is believed to be the nearest living terrestrial relative. A fourth species of manatee, Steller's sea cow, was hunted to extinction in 1786.

The Sirenia is the only order of aquatic herbivorous mammal (no other aquatic mammals are solely herbivores) and are found in warm, shallow, coastal waters such as swamps, estuaries and rivers. They live on a diet of sea grass and other marine vegetation but a gradual loss of habitat, often the result of property developments compromising their ecosystem, and the growing prevalence of leisure activities such as powerboating, has endangered all of these species. Neither do their natural characteristics – a slow metabolism and unhurried response to danger – help them help themselves.

Sirenians have evolved a physique which is both streamlined and highly muscular. Their forelimbs are modified arms used for steering while their hind limbs have all but disappeared, retained only as two small functionless bones. The tail acts as a powerful paddle and rudder – essential assets for a creature that can grow up to 4 m (13 ft) long and weigh as much as 1,500 kg (3,307 lb)

Over eons the bones of these mammals have become extremely dense in order to counter-balance the buoyancy of their blubber. This trade-off allows them to maneuver better in a three-dimensional environment and their huge lung capacity and strong diaphragm allows them to stay underwater for prolonged periods. They have only two teats under their forelimbs to suckle their young and, like cetaceans, never leave the water to give birth. The skull is adapted for taking in air at the water's surface while their teeth are short, blunt and quickly renewed at the front of the mouth as older teeth are worn down.

▶ *Dugong use their distinctively shaped mouths to forage for sea grass.*

▼ *Propeller cuts are clearly visible on the tail of this West Indian manatee.*

▲ *West Indian manatees swim in the shallow waters of Florida's Crystal River.*

Manatees

There are three species of manatee; the West Indian (*Trichechus manatus*), the West African (*T. Senegalensis*) and the Amazonian (*T. Inunguis*). Manatees migrate to find food and, because they are completely herbivorous, are found in shallow waters where the plants they eat can easily photosynthesize. They are large, ponderous mammals who like to munch marine vegetation as they swim through it at a steady 4–8 km (2.5–5 miles) per hour. When pushed, though, they can hit short bursts of up to 32 km (20 miles) per hour.

▼ *An Amazon manatee adult emerges from the water to graze on the riverbank vegetation.*

The US population is estimated at about 3,800, most of which spend summer in the southern states of Alabama, Georgia and South Carolina before migrating to Florida in winter. West Indian manatees are found around coastal and inland waterways along the northern and eastern coasts of South America, eastern Mexico, Central America and the Greater Antilles. Although mostly coastal creatures they can thrive in brackish or fresh water and can live for up to 60 years where their habitat is undisturbed. However, they cannot tolerate colder waters.

The West African manatee is similar to its West Indian cousin in size and nature although comparatively little is known of this animal given the dearth of detailed studies carried out in African waters. The smaller, Amazonian species lives, as its name suggests, in the River Amazon and its tributaries feeding on freshwater vegetation. Its distinguishing features include a smooth skin and an absence of nails on its flippers.

Manatees consume up to 15 per cent of their body weight daily, surfacing to breathe every three to five minutes while eating and staying submerged for up to 20 minutes while resting on the bottom. Females are not sexually mature until the age of about five. They gestate for a year or so, then produce a single calf (very occasionally twins) every two to five years which they suckle for another couple of years. Males become sexually active slightly earlier – from perhaps three years onwards.

▲ *A Dugong swims over a coral reef near Epi Island in the Pacific Ocean.*

On the edge of extinction – the dugong

Dugongs (*Dugong dugon*) live across a wide geographic area including the warm coastal waters of the Pacific and Indian oceans and the Red Sea. The largest population is found along Australia's northern coastline between Shark Bay and Moreton Bay while the second largest is found in the Arabian Gulf. But the notion of a large population is highly relative; dugongs were hunted for years for their meat, skin, bones and oil and are now a seriously endangered and internationally protected species.

To the casual observer they differ from their close cousins the manatees by having a powerful, flat-fluked tail, rather like a whale's, which propels them powerfully through the water. They use their flippers for steering, have no hind legs, and their brown skin is stubbled with short, thick hair. Their thick blubber layer gives them a rounded profile and the blunt head has two nostrils lodged on a fleshy lip which can be curled up to make breathing easier. They grow small tusks; obvious in males but usually concealed in the gums of females.

Dugongs use their sensitive mouths to snuffle and root around for underwater grasses to munch with their rough 'lips'. They can happily eat around the clock but have to surface for air every six minutes or so, a requirement that sometimes sees them apparently standing on their tails, their heads poking above the water like curious seals. They grow up to 3 m (10 ft) long, weigh anything up to 500 kg (1,100 lb) and can live for 70 years in the right environment. Much of this time is spent alone, or with their mate, although they are known to gather together in herds where larger populations are established.

Sexual maturity arrives between the ages of 10 and 17, with females giving birth every three to seven years. A calf is carried in the womb for 12 months and once it emerges into the water the mother immediately propels it to the surface to take its first breath. Suckling with milk continues for between 18 and 24 months before mother and calf go their separate ways.

These slow-moving, docile animals would make a tasty meal for many predators but fortunately their immense size is a deterrent to most. Only killer whlaes, larger sharks and crocodiles are big enough to threaten them.

▶ *Dugong use their powerful, whale-like tails to propel them through the water.*

Marine carnivores

The marine animals of the order Carnivora are thought to be largely descended from meat-eating terrestrial ancestors – hence their thick furry coats (sea otters and polar bears have the thickest). They are divided into three main families; the Pinnipedia, Mustelidae and Ursidae. Of these the Pinnipedia is by far the largest and most obvious place to begin our introduction.

The Pinnipedia family

This 'super-family' comprises finned mammals with torpedo-shaped bodies superbly equipped for cutting through the water. They are aquatic but can spend significant periods on land where they give birth to their young. They have a global distribution, mostly coastal waters where they feed on mollusks, fish and other aquatic animals and have adapted to ocean life with strong, elongated 'hands' and 'feet' terminating in digits bound by tough webbing. Their teeth are like small pegs while tails are rudimentary affairs almost ancillary to steering.

◄ *A Hawaiian monk seal mother enjoys the surf with her pup.*

▼ *They may belong to the same marine order, but seal is a favorite food for the polar bear.*

The Pinnipedia (its name comes from the Latin pinna, meaning 'wing' or 'feather' and pedis, meaning 'foot') is sub-divided into three groups. These are the Phocidae (about 18 species of true or 'earless' seals), the Otariidae (some 16 types of eared seal) and the Odobenidae (a single species of walrus).

The Phocidae

The Phocidae 'true' or 'earless' seals have a global population spread across polar, sub-polar and temperate waters, the only exception being monk seals (*Monachus* spp.) which occupy the tropics. These species all have sleek, streamlined bodies offering outstanding speed and maneuverability in water and they spend most of their lives in the oceans, venturing ashore only to mate or give birth. While eared seals such as the fur seal have their evolutionary roots in a terrestrial bear it is thought that the likes of the common or harbor seal (*Phoca vitulina*) are descended from an ancient version of the otter.

True seals have a wonderfully hydrodynamic profile; not only have they dispensed with external ears they have managed to ditch all external features which aren't absolutely necessary to their survival. Reproductive organs are all located internally and females can even retract their nipples in the cause of reduced friction. Beneath their skin lies a thick layer of blubber into which seals can divert blood flow – a remarkably efficient temperature regulator. All this means that true seals can swim further and for longer than their eared cousins and consequently can be found living happily far out into the world's oceans.

True seals can also dive to considerable depths and stay submerged for long periods while they hunt for food. In fact the northern elephant seal (*Mirounga angustirostris*) can remain underwater for up to half an hour before rapidly re-surfacing, taking in air for two or three minutes and heading back to the depths. To avoid the risk of decompression sickness (a condition known as the 'bends' in which nitrogen bubbles form in the blood as the result of a quick ascent) these animals have a middle ear lined with blood sinuses which inflate during dives and help stabilize pressure. When at depth air is forced into the upper respiratory passages where oxygen cannot easily be absorbed into the blood stream.

On land these seals are ungainly, relying on the flexing of their stomach muscles and the use of fore flippers to clumsily propel themselves. Unlike their cousin the walrus they can't turn their hind flippers under their body to attempt a form of 'walking' on all fours. But once in the water they are transformed into fast, agile swimmers powering themselves with hind flippers and steering with the front ones to produce a gloriously sinuous motion. Communication appears fairly primitive – essentially grunts and flipper slapping.

Species of true seals vary considerably in size; the ringed seal (*Pusa hispida*) for instance is around 1.17 m (3.8 ft) and 45 kg (99 lb) whereas the biggest of all Phocidae, the southern elephant seal (*Mirounga leonina*), can weigh in at a bullish 2,400 kg (5,291 lb) and grow to 4.9 m (16 ft) in length.

Pregnant true seals can be found foraging far out across the oceans in a determined effort to build up the huge reserves of fat necessary for their confinement on breeding or 'nursery' sites, which are often hundreds of kilometers from their usual hunting grounds. The birth and suckling process is one of nature's enduring miracles; remarkably the mother is able to produce high-calorie milk from her stored fat while managing herself without food and, usually, without water as well.

◄ A southern elephant seal
bull emerges from the surf off
South Georgia Island in the
southern Atlantic Ocean.

The milk is designed to be so thick and fat-rich that the pup can take on massive amounts of nutrition and energy in the shortest possible time. This allows the mother to return to the sea, hunt and feed, and restore her own strength before sustaining any lasting damage. The time scale for this process varies considerably. The hooded seal (*Cystophora cristata*) for instance manages it in between three to five days while for the northern elephant seal it can take up to 28 days.

The pup fattens up quickly and by the time its mother leaves it can live off its own fat reserves for weeks (up to 12 weeks in the case of the northern elephant seal) while learning to hunt and kill for itself. This period is known as the 'fast' and during this time the pup is unlikely to eat or even drink while its body matures. Most Phocidae species have few teeth although hunting is aided by the retention of powerful canines.

Population levels are generally healthy with the exception of two types of monk seal. The Hawaiian monk seal (*Monachus schauinsland*) which inhabits the tropical waters of the Hawaiian archipelago is seriously endangered (barely a thousand survive) but its future is at least more certain than its cousin the Mediterranean seal (*M. Monachus*) whose numbers are down to perhaps 400 individuals. If anyone is in any doubt about the huge threat facing these two species it is worth bearing in mind the recent fate of the Caribbean monk seal (*M. tropicalis*), declared extinct in 2008.

▼ *The Hawaiian monk seal is among the most endangered of all seal species.*

The Otariidae

The Otariidae – better known as 'eared seals' – is a sizeable family of 16 very similar species which encompasses both fur seals and sea lions. These animals breed and rest on land or ice, taking to the water mainly to hunt and migrate. The differences between some of them are so slight that scientists investigating their morphology have reclassified several species and drawn new familial lines. Other than having external ears, the biggest difference between them and their cousins the 'true seals' lies in the way they independently control their hind flippers – an enormous help to mobility on land – and swim using their large fore flippers. In the water these flippers power the animal forward while the rear ones provide balance and direction. As you might expect, all otariids have a layer of blubber for effective insulation in colder waters.

Otariidae are coastally distributed around North and South America, central and northern Asia, various Pacific islands, New Zealand, and the Indian Ocean along the south west coast of Australia. They tend to be social, herd-forming animals which gather in large numbers (especially during the breeding season) on remote beaches, rocky coastlines and caves. However, some species, notably the sea lions, can become aggressive during the breeding season.

Otariids possess the characteristics of all seals – fast and powerful in the water with perfectly streamlined bodies. They have dog-like heads with small, external ear flaps and have a unique claim to fame within the animal kingdom. Males can be proportionately up to six times bigger than the female of the species, giving otariids the greatest difference in size and weight between males and females of the same species (sexual diamorphism).

These animals breed annually, usually at the rate of one pup per year - the only exception being the Australian sea lion (*Neophoca cinerea*) which breeds every 17.5 months. Typically otariids migrate annually to hereditary breeding grounds (rookeries), in well-defined seasons, to play out one of the natural world's most compelling social spectacles.

The males arrive first where they ostentatiously display their attributes to potential rivals and fight to claim the best territory. When the females turn up the mature males collect and jealously guard as many as they can, fighting off other suitors who try to get too close. The strongest, most aggressive, males assemble the largest harems – perhaps 40 females, which will give birth within days of joining. These pups will have been gestated for 10–12 months since the last breeding season, making use of a biological process known as delayed implantation, in which gestation is put on hold for a period of up to four months, before pups start to develop again in utero. Within a few days the females regain fertility and within 12 days mate again, triggering a new life cycle. Once nursing of the young is complete all the animals return to the sea until the following year's breeding season.

◀ *A colony of South American sea lions and South American fur seals at the Point Coles Nature Reserve in Peru.*

▼ *The Galapagos fur seal spends approximately 70 per cent of its life in the water.*

▲ *Steller sea lions –
like all members of the
Otariidae family – are
very sociable creatures.*

◀ *The Antarctic
fur seal is perfectly
adapted to life in the
freezing waters.*

Otariidae have long, sensitive whiskers used both as low-light sensors to seek out food and also to avoid predators. They attack prey with sharp teeth, including well-developed canines, are active day and night and hunt around the clock for fish, krill, cephalopods, mollusks, crustaceans and even penguins. Their hunting range is extensive, from the ocean's surface down to the deepest reaches and they have a voracious appetite. Even a small fur seal weighing 50 kg (110 lb) will consume between 1.8 and 2.3 kg (4–5 lb) of food every feeding time.

Fur seals are all members of the polar genus Arctocephalus but the northern fur seal (*Callorhinus ursinus*) is the only species in the northern hemisphere (eight are found in the southern). The smallest member of the family is the Galapagos fur seal (*A. galapagoensis*) at about 70 kg (150 lb) while the largest is the enormous Steller sea lion (*Eumetopias jubatus*), aka northern sea lion, with males which tip the scales at an average 907 kg (2,000 lb) and grow up to 2.1 m (7 ft) long.

Collectively a member of the fur seals group, sea lions are classified as five species of Otariidae; a sixth, the Japanese sea lion (*Zalophus japonicus*) is thought to have become extinct in the 1960s.

They differ from the other fur seals by their enormous physical bulk and lack of thick underfur; instead their fur is formed from short, coarse, hair.

Sea lions are opportunistic predators, particularly of cephalopods and fish, but Steller sea lions will eat other seals given half the chance. All mammals in this group like to seek out upwellings in coastal waters where nutrient-rich waters attract a vast array of tasty marine life.

The Steller sea lion lives in two distinct areas of the North Pacific; an eastern population around southern Alaska, British Columbia and California and a western grouping around Japan, the Bering Sea and Gulf of Alaska. Male Stellers, characterized by their thick bull neck and rough mane of fur, mature at between three and eight years old but will not grow to sufficient bulk and strength until nine or ten when they can fight off rivals and mate successfully. Females mature sexually aged between four and six years when they bear a single pup and quickly seek to mate again. Mother and pup stay together for about a year.

▼ *A group of South American sea lions cavort in Argentinean waters.*

Unfortunately these enormous animals face a real battle for survival, especially the Steller, Australian and Galapagos (*Zalophus wollebaeki*) species, while the New Zealand sea lion (*Phocarctos hookeri*) is now classified as vulnerable.

The Odobenidae

The walrus (*Odobenus rosmarus*) is the sole member of the Odobenidae family and lives in shallow waters and floating ice from the Arctic Sea to the northern latitudes of the Pacific and Atlantic. The global population is estimated at around 250,000, four fifths of which are Pacific-based. There are three subspecies; the Pacific walrus (*Odobenus rosmarus divergens*), the Atlantic walrus (*O.rosmarus rosmarus*) and the Laptev Sea walrus (*O.rosmarus laptevi*).

Walruses are large, tusked, reddish-brown, furry mammals copiously equipped with some distinctive whiskers, scientifically called mystacial vibrissae. Together these form a delicate sensory organ (see Otariidae above). They have no obvious ears and their fore flippers are short and square-shaped with tiny claws at the ends of the digits; hind flippers are triangular with three large claws on each. Both males and females are tusked – actually elongated canine teeth – and the male's can reach 1 m (3.3 ft) long and weigh 5.4 kg (12 lb). These present a fearsome defensive weapon, not to be taken lightly by occasional predators such as polar bears and orcas, but they are also used for mating display rituals and scouring holes in the ice. Typically, the male with the strongest tusks will become the dominant animal – normally living for between 20 and 30 years.

The walrus's heavy, wrinkled skin covers a solid layer of blubber up to 15 cm (5.9 in) thick. This acts both as an insulator and a buoyancy aid and, as an additional safeguard for the long nights at sea, further buoyancy is provided by a large air sac under the throat which helps the animal sleep safely, its head bobbing above the waves.

On land and sea ice walruses blunder around on all four flippers, their hind limbs rotated beneath their pelvic girdle to make walking easier. Pacific walruses are about ten per cent larger than Atlantic ones and the males of both subspecies are larger than the females, up to 3.6 m (12 ft) long in the male and a maximum of 3.1 m (10 ft) in the female. Males typically weigh in at around 1,700 kg (3,748 lb) as opposed to the female maximum of around 1,250 kg (2,756 lb). All being well they can live for up to 30 years.

Walruses live on a diet of bivalve mollusks, especially clams, along with fish, marine worms, snails, squid, sea cucumber, soft corals and crabs (although they will also scavenge seal carcasses when they get the chance). They can remain submerged for up to half an hour in their search for food and prefer to target shallow, coastal sea beds. This inevitably disturbs silt and sediment and performs a valuable function for other marine animals by re-circulating nutrients into the water.

The female walrus becomes sexually mature by the age of about six but is unlikely to pup before ten. She will gestate for some 16 months before giving birth to a single pup of about 60 kg (132 lb) during the spring migration between April and

◄ *They may look cumbersome on land, but the walrus is truly in its element in the water, as this adult female demonstrates.*

▲ *Two Pacific walrus bulls fight in shallow water in the Bering Sea, Alaska.*

June. The young are suckled and weaned over a period of two years or so but calves stay with their mothers for a further three years – including the late summer migration when tens of thousands of walruses gather together on rocky outcrops and beaches in preparation for their return journey.

Although the female may successfully mate she will delay ovulation (and subsequent pregnancy) until her calf has weaned. This means that, at best, a mature female can give birth only once every two years and makes the walrus the slowest-reproducing pinniped of all. Males mature from the age of eight, though do not usually successfully mate for a further seven years. The rut lasts from January until April, during which time the males virtually stop eating as they fight to defend their females and territory from intruders.

▼ *A parent with its young pup float on an ice floe off the coast of Norway.*

The mustelidae family

The Mustelidae family provides the largest group of Carnivora
and contains terrestrial animals such as weasels, polecats,
badgers and minks. But only one branch of the family, the
Lutrinae, includes marine mammals. These are sea otters,
sometime known as marine weasels, and they are further
divided into three subspecies. The first is the common or Asian
sea otter (*Enhydra lutris lutris*) – the largest marine otter,
easily recognizable from its short, blunt nose on a wide skull
and found from the Russian Kuril islands in the north western
Pacific to the Commander Islands in the Bering Sea.

▲ *A marine otter struggles in
the water with a catch that is
larger than the hunter itself.*

Secondly there is the southern or Californian sea otter
(*E.L. nereis*) found off the central Californian coast; this has
a narrower, more characteristic otter skull with small teeth.
Finally we have the northern sea otter (*E.L. kenyoni*), which
inhabits the coastal waters of Alaska and the Pacific west
coast as far down as Washington. With considerable help
from conservationists this animal's range is slowly extending
southwards.

A near relative is the rare and elusive marine otter (*Lontra felina*), which belongs to the *Lontra* genus of American river otters. It lives in sea caves along the wild and rocky shorelines of Chile, southern Peru and the extreme south of Argentina. Smaller than sea otters, and with coarser fur, marine otters have been hunted extensively and are now mostly protected, although they are still poached in more remote areas. Numbers are unknown but are estimated to be around the thousand mark.

Another cousin, the sea mink (*Neovison macrodon*), was hunted to extinction in 1860 for its much-prized pelt. Very little is known of its habits but it lived in the coastal waters of the rocky Atlantic littoral of Canada and New England and was altogether larger than its cousin the American mink (*N. vision*).

The threat to both marine and sea otters grew rapidly with the development of the commercial fur trade in the 18th century and by the mid 20th century the sea otter population was barely 1,000. Since then an international hunting ban, and conservation strategies such as reintroduction programs, have helped them recover. However the sea otter remains firmly on the endangered species list.

The battle to ensure its survival is not simply about the need to protect a rare animal, important though that is. The sea otter is a 'keystone' species; in other words it is fundamentally critical to its habitat and the well-being of other life forms existing there. A good example is the otter's voracious appetite for sea urchins which could otherwise devastate kelp forest ecosystems and all marine life dependent upon them.

Otters are the smallest marine mammal with mature male adults weighing anything between 18 and 45 kg (40-99 lb) and growing to between 1.2 and 1.5 m (4-5 ft). Females are somewhat lighter at 14–33 kg (30–73 lb) and grow between 1 and 1.4 m (3.3-4.7 ft). Both sexes spend most of their time at sea, living on average between 15 and 20 years, although they can be quite agile on the few occasions they set a paw on land.

Uniquely among marine mammals the sea otter has no blubber for insulation against the cold and instead possesses the thickest and densest fur coat anywhere in the animal kingdom – around one million strands of hair per 6.45 square centimeters (1 square inch). The coat consists of two layers; the outer, long, waterproof guard hairs prevent water from reaching the shorter, dense underfur. This remarkable arrangement gives the otter a much plumper appearance than is actually the case.

Because it depends so heavily on its fur to survive, the sea otter understandably devotes a huge amount of time to grooming. This includes blowing air into the pelt to keep it absolutely clean and waterproof, a process which has required the animal to evolve surprisingly supple limbs as a way of reaching every part of its body for deep-down attention. Fur is continuously shed and replaced – eliminating any risk of vulnerability to cold during a molt – and the habit of meticulous grooming is bestowed on cubs from a very early age – witness the time mother otters take in cleaning their cubs.

Otters have developed additional marine attributes, such as closing their nostrils and ears and using highly-sensitive whiskers to find prey in the dark. The short front paws have tough pads and retractable claws which are used to catch and grasp prey – unlike other marine carnivores they catch their food with their forepaws and then tear at it with their teeth. The sea otter has a huge lung capacity, over twice that of land mammals, and can remain submerged for up to five minutes. This is no mean feat when you consider that a combination of full lungs and air trapped in its fur makes the animal highly buoyant.

▼ *A sea otter dives into a kelp forest to forage for food.*

Sea otters are active during the day and sleep for most of the night. Typically, they wake soon after sunrise and immediately forage for food, taking a few hours nap or rest around midday. This resting period often sees them floating chest-up on the water, perhaps holding a fish or minding a pup, before resuming the search for food. After a further break they may sometimes embark on a third hunting expedition, around midnight, before finally entering their main sleep period. To prevent themselves drifting away while sleeping or eating they have developed the knack of entwining themselves in long strands of sea kelp.

Most of the animal's food sources are found on the sea floor during a series of short dives (perhaps four minutes) during which it lifts and turns over boulders to see what morsels lie beneath. It will then store its catch in a loose pouch of skin extending under its forepaws across its chest. Back on the surface it rolls over, pulls the catch from its pouch and tears the food apart with its paws to eat at leisure. Particular favorites are marine invertebrates such as molluscs, sea urchins and crustaceans as well as some types of fish. In hunting the latter, otters can reach speeds of up to 9 kph (5.6 mph) propelled by long, broad, fully-webbed hind feet and a thick, muscular, slightly flattened tail.

Unusually for a marine creature the sea otter uses tools, often grabbing a stone with its forepaws to hammer favored shellfish such as oysters and abalone off the rocks before smashing them open. It has been estimated that in cold temperatures sea otters need to eat up to 35 per cent of their body weight every day to stay insulated from the cold. However, drinking is not a problem; they sip sea water which their large kidneys turn into fresh, leaving salts to be excreted in highly-concentrated urine.

Although individuals spend a lot of time alone hunting and sleeping they also congregate in groups or 'rafts' of single-sex animals numbering up to 100. Males become sexually mature at about five years old and between spring and autumn establish their territory, mating with any females which venture onto their patch. Most otters breed in the autumn but the pair-bonding lasts only a few days and females, which are sexually mature by the age of three, can delay implantation, in a similar manner to the Otariidae. This means that, while pregnancy itself last 4 months, gestation can vary between 4 and 12 months.

▼ *Three adult sea otters take a rest, floating on their backs during the heat of the day.*

Pups can be born at any time but mostly between May and June in the northern populations and January and March in the south. Californian sea otters usually breed every year while the Alaskan follows a two-year cycle. But in all cases the pups are born at sea, almost always singletons, and are covered with an extremely buoyant baby fur that ensures they bob around in the water with no danger of drowning. This infant fur lasts for some 13 weeks, after which the pup can learn to swim and dive. Mothers nurse their young for between 6 and 12 months, providing the pups with sustaining, high-fat milk.

▶ *A sea otter takes time out to float in the water with its pup.*

▼ *A sea otter eating a crab off the California coast.*

MOLLUSKS

From tiny sea snails to the giant squid, on the face of it there's very little that's uniform about mollusks. In fact they share something of a common body plan. Naturalists who realized it named them mollusks, meaning 'soft animals', derived from *mollis*, the Latin word for soft.

There's an array of apparent contradictions surrounding them. The species which grow external shells range from tiny snails of around 2 to 3 mm (0.08–0.1 in) to the giant clam (*Tridacna gigas*); this can grow to enormous sizes – there is a museum specimen which measures 137 cm (4 ft 5 in) long and weighs 263 kg (580 lb).

While most mollusks are either immobile or can only move very slowly, others, such as the members of the Cephalopoda, are capable of great speed. The biggest member of mollusk family is the colossal squid (*Mesonychoteuthis hamiltoni*), which can reach lengths of up to 14 m (46 ft).

Most mollusks live in marine environments, but they also occur in fresh water as well as on land. There are something like 112,000 species of mollusk known to exist; however, it is highly likely that many more will be discovered in the ocean depths.

Given the number of species and the variety of shapes and sizes, scientists have had their work cut out in assigning them to eight classes of mollusk, including Polyplacophora (chitons), Bivalvia (bivalves), Scaphopoda (tusk shells), Gastropoda (univalves or snails) and Cephalopoda (octopus, squid and cuttlefish).

◀ *Giant clam populations are diminishing quickly and the clam has become extinct in many areas where it was once common.*

Marine mollusks feed on a wide variety of different things. Many, including limpets, periwinkles and chitons, consume vegetation and static prey. As they don't have to pounce on prey, they tend to be slow-moving and well-armored to protect against attack. Depending on the species, they feed on a variety of plant matter, ranging from microscopic algae to large fronds of kelp. In order to do this, they have a rasp-like tongue called a radula. Many other mollusks are filter feeders that sieve microscopic creatures such as plankton from the water around them – these include bivalves like mussels and scallops.

The majority of mollusks are predators; some of these are quite obviously so. Squid, cuttlefish and octopus are all well-known for their ability to catch and consume prey. Many seashell species, however, are also efficient hunter-killers.

Most of the cone shells, for instance, are equipped with barbed harpoon-like structures that contain powerful toxins. These are used when hunting fish, marine worms or other molluscs. Some of the poisons involved are strong enough to kill an adult human – examples include the geography cone (*Conus geographus*), the cat cone (*Conus catus*), the tulip cone (*Conus tulipa*) and the striated cone (*Conus striatus*). The most deadly of the cone mollusks have enough venom in a single sting to kill up to 70 adults. There's no anti-venom known to man. Other species are also able to deliver very nasty stings that can cause breathing difficulties, paralysis and other side effects. It has been discovered that these creatures can

▲ *The geography cone has the most toxic sting known among Conus species and is responsible for more than 30 human fatalities.*

be used for a range of painkillers more powerful than morphine.

Mollusk eggs may be laid singly or in large masses. When they hatch, they do so as one of three different forms, depending on the species concerned. The first two types are known as trochophores and veligers, larval forms that join the vast mass of open water plankton until they are ready to develop into the adult stage. The third kind has a direct form of development, hatching from the egg into tiny replicas of the adults.

▶ *California two-spot octopus juveniles hatch from their egg cases.*

Gastropods

The gastropod class includes land snails, slugs and sea slugs, as well as the majority of the single-shelled seashell species. About 70,000 to 75,000 species have been described scientifically, although the figure cannot be exact at this stage due to changes in the taxonomic classification and because of difficulties with identification.

All have a spiral twist to their bodies which is referred to as 'torsion'. Oddly, this leaves their anus above their heads, posing an obvious difficulty with waste clearance. However, despite this, the species has proliferated.

Most gastropods have a special trapdoor-like structure called an operculum which they are able to open and close at will. This is used for a number of different purposes, but the most important is to keep out predators. Those species in tidal zones also use it to prevent drying out at low tide. Marine gastropods feed on many different things including plants such as algae and seaweed, decaying animal or vegetative matter, or they may be active hunters of live prey. They are able to move around freely using a powerful muscular foot, with hunters typically being faster than the plant browsers. They have varying degrees of vision and usually have eyes at the tips of tentacles which project forward from the head.

Gastropods can be found in a wide variety of different habitats, with some hidden from view after burrowing into mud or sand. Others, such as limpets, live on rocks in full view and rely on hard armor for protection against the wind, waves and predators.

One of the suborders or 'clades' of the gastropods are the nudibranchs, commonly known as sea slugs. Around 3,000 different species have been recorded and, although most of these are relatively small, some can reach as much as 600 mm in length. Over time they have dispensed with their protective shells. Instead, many have evolved effective chemical defenses which are composed of powerful toxins derived from the substances contained in the creatures they have been eating.

They usually parade the fact that they are inedible with a display of bright warning colors in spectacular patterns.

▼ *A Purple-ring top snail attacks a cluster of strawberry anemone.*

Many other creatures in the local environment, such as flatworms, impersonate the coloration to take advantage of the protection it offers. This effect, which is known as Batesian mimicry, can bestow substantial advantages on those that can carry it off effectively.

It is not the only device used by sea slugs, however. Others eschew lurid colors in favor of camouflage, developing color schemes that closely match the surrounding corals or seaweeds. This is made easier because they reuse many of the pigments they have ingested from the plants they have been feeding on. The colors derived in this way are even used to provide extra camouflage for the eggs in some species. A few sea slugs have gone even further and are able to relocate the green chloroplasts from photosynthetic plants into their body tissues. This not only gives them a cryptic coloration, but also the benefit of an extra supply of nutrients from the sun's energy. Other species are almost transparent – this means that they are able to blend in with their backgrounds very well.

Most of the many species of sea slug acquire oxygen via feathery gills. These are often both complex and elegant structures. A few species, however, simply breathe directly through the skin.

Most are predators, attacking and eating barnacles, sponges, hydroids and bryozoans. A few, however, are hunters of other sea slugs.

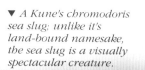

▼ *A Kune's chromodoris sea slug: unlike it's land-bound namesake, the sea slug is a visually spectacular creature.*

▲ *The name sea hare derive from their rounded shape and the two long rhinophores that project upwards from their heads that resemble rabbit ears.*

Polyplacophora

The chitons, also known as coat-of-mail shells, are an interesting group of limpet-like creatures that belong to the class Polyplacophora. They can sometimes be found in on the shoreline attached to the undersides of rocks. The class contains around a thousand different species, all of which are exclusively marine. Most inhabit shallow coastal areas, but a small number are known to live at great depths. Their shells are articulated, being made up of eight plates that fit closely together. These allow the shell to arch or curve so it will fit closely against a range of contoured surfaces. Unlike limpets, which have to remain close to a specific resting site that fits their shell, it means that chitons are able move around much more freely. Chitons usually feed on the various kinds of microscopic algae that grow on rocks, as well as diatoms and bryozoans. A few, however, are able to catch and eat fish or small invertebrates. Chitons reproduce after sperm and eggs are released into the water. A few species brood a fertile egg while one species gives birth to live young. Most chitons are quite small, measuring between 20 and 40 mm (0.8–1.6 in), but some can grow quite large, with the biggest being the giant Pacific chiton (Cryptochiton stelleri), which can reach 33 cm (13 in) in length.

◄ *A blue-lined chiton uses its radula to scrape food from substrate.*

► *A queen scallop swims to escape an attack by common starfish.*

▼ *The fan mussel is one of the largest European bivalve mollusks. It is one of the rarest species of marine mollusk in the United Kingdom.*

Bivalves

Mollusks that have two separate parts to their shell are known as bivalves. Common examples include mussels, scallops and clams. There are currently around 30,000 known species, all of which are filter feeders, surviving on floating particles or microscopic creatures. Some, such as the swan mussel, are found in fresh water, but the vast majority live in marine environments.

Among the bivalves, there are three basic lifestyle categories. Some species are sessile – that is, they attach themselves permanently to a home using a number of strong threads known as a byssus onto a suitable substrate, such as a rock, a pier stanchion, or some other fixed structure. This is what mussels do.

Others burrow into sand, mud, submerged wood, or soft rock, making tunnels in which they subsequently live. The shipworms are well-known wood-borers, and, as the name would suggest, they can be a major problem for wooden boats. Razor shells and cockles are among the many species that dig themselves into sand.

The third group of bivalves is comprised of the species that are capable of swimming freely – these include scallops, which are excellent swimmers who will rise up from the sea bed and quickly swim away if they feel threatened.

◄ *The shell of the chambered nautilus exhibits countershading, being light on the bottom and dark on top to confuse potential predators both above and below.*

Cambrian Period, well before vertebrates such as fish evolved. For vast periods of time they were the dominant life forms in the world's seas and oceans. Unlike their close relations the slugs and snails, they evolved tentacles or arms in place of the more typical molluscan muscular foot. As a result, all the cephalopods have excellent manual dexterity. Combined with their superb vision and high levels of intelligence, this makes them fearsome predators. The cephalopods have highly unusual internal organs: they have three hearts which work together to circulate their blue-colored blood.

The six species of nautilus are the only living members of the class to have retained a shell. They form an ancient genus, having ancestors that stretch back into the fossil record. They are nocturnal, and swim freely in the waters of the Indian and south-western Pacific Oceans. During the day they sink to depths of between 160 and 330 m (525–1080 ft), but under cover of darkness they move towards the surface to hunt for prey using their long tentacles. The females lay eggs once a year on rocks in shallow coastal areas during a life span that can last for up to 20 years or so, which is an unusually long time for cephalopods.

With its eight powerful arms, the octopus is easy to identify. However, when it comes to specifics there are problems. There are nearly 300 different species of octopus and almost all of them are soft-bodied predators of one sort or another. As they do not have any hard body parts, they are able to squeeze through very narrow gaps. They use this ability to good effect when hunting or seeking safe shelter. A small number of deep water species retain the remnants of an internal shell, but they live in environments where they do not have to chase prey or evade capture by hiding in closely confined spaces. Using a parrot-like beak they can make short work of prey and are known for being the most intelligent of the mollusks. Two different species vie with one another for the title of the largest octopus. These are the North Pacific giant octopus (*Enteroctopus dofleini*), and the seven-arm octopus (*Haliphron atlanticus*). This last species in fact has the requisite eight arms but one is normally curled up and hidden. Both have been recorded at weights of around 70 kg (150 lb).

Cephalopods

Cephalopods are exclusively marine, and can be found in all the major seas and oceans, inhabiting every level from the shallows to the extreme depths. They have superb vision thanks to a highly developed pair of eyes. They also have large brains, and are thought to be the most intelligent of all the invertebrates.

In the modern era, the Cephalopoda class comprises creatures that are generally well-known – these are the squid, cuttlefish, nautilus and octopus, of which there are almost 88 species. In the millions of years before the dinosaur evolved, however, there were many more. Although their soft bodies do not preserve well, there are still around 11,000 species known from the fossil record. The first examples probably appeared in the late

◄ *The greater blue-ringed octopus, a small but extremely poisonous animal; one individual contains enough venom to kill twenty adults.*

However, there are numerous but unconfirmed reports of much bigger specimens.

Like the other cephalopods, cuttlefish are highly intelligent. They have eight arms, two tentacles, and excellent vision. Voracious hunters, they can hunt either individually or in packs. Their favorite meal is small marine creatures, such as shrimps, prawns, fish and crustaceans. Nick-named the chameleon of the sea, their skin has many thousands of special cells called chromatophores. These allow the cuttlefish to change their color whenever they want to and this can be done at great speed. Color changes are used both for camouflage as well as a highly advanced visual communication system. They are preyed upon by a wide variety of marine creatures, including sharks, dolphins and seals, as well as humans. They have an internal shell that is known as a cuttlebone – these are widely used in the pet trade to provide calcium for caged birds.

Various species of squid are found throughout the seas and oceans of the world, where they are efficient predators of fish and other small creatures. Like their close relations the cuttlefish, squid have eight arms, two tentacles and excellent sight. Instead of having an internal cuttlebone skeleton, however, they have a stiff clear structure made from a material that resembles plastic, called a 'pen'. They also have chromatophoric skin which is used for camouflage and communication. Squid are able to move around very quickly due to an unusual feature called the siphon. This is a narrow duct through which a high pressure jet of water can be squirted. The direction and size of the jet can be carefully modulated providing an effective means of high speed propulsion. When they are threatened, squid are able to expel a cloud of dark ink from a storage organ. This hides them from view while they escape and confuses the predator.

▶ *The toxin of the flamboyant cuttlefish has been discovered to be as toxic as that of the blue-ringed octopus.*

▶ *The bigfin reef squid tend to remain close to the shoreline and are extremely sensitive to chemical changes in the water.*

MARINE WORMS

Pits and troughs that cover the sea bed are a clue to the existence of an ocean resident that's rarely seen but frequently leaves a telltale calling card.

There are a multitude of worms living in marine environments yet they are rarely spotted even by the most ardent ocean user. Only disturbances in the sand caused by their burrowing or the piles of excrement they leave behind point to their presence. These are grouped into a variety of phyla, classes and genera, and include numerous examples.

Horseshoe worms

Phoronids, which are sometimes referred to as horseshoe worms, live on the sea bed in tubes made from special secretions. Often in large colonies, they prefer relatively shallow water – typically down to depths of 70 m (230 ft) or so – in all the seas and oceans except those in the polar regions. The twenty known species range in size from 6 mm (0.25 in) up to around 50 cm (20 in) in length and live for about a year.

▼ *A star horseshoe worm growing in hump coral in waters 40 feet deep around the Solomon Islands.*

Roundworms

The nematodes are an enormous and extremely diverse phylum of worm-like creatures (commonly called roundworms), with over 28,000 species known to science. Undoubtedly, there are many more still waiting to be discovered. Some estimates put the final total at as many as half a million. To illustrate their numerical superiority, a study off the coast of Holland claimed 4.4 million nematodes in just one square meter (10.8 square feet). They can be found in almost every possible habitat, from tropical rainforests to the frozen wastes of the polar regions, and from the tops of mountains to the deepest reaches of the oceans. Indeed, it has been estimated that around 90 per of the life found on the sea bed is composed of nematodes. More than half of those which have been documented are parasitic. Nematodes are round, slender, elongated and tapered at both ends. They feed on small animals and have shown cannibalistic inclinations when food gets short. Most species are hermaphrodites although a few are gender specific.

Acorn worms

The class called Enteropneusta – better known as acorn worms – embraces about 70 species of creature that occur in marine environments down to depths of about 3,000 m (10,000 ft) They are largely stationary animals that often contain compounds of bromine to deter predators. The only sense

organs they have are situated in front of the mouth, taking the form of a large proboscis. These are probably used to taste the water for traces of food and to collect it. Small body hairs called cilia transport the food from the proboscis to the mouth. This same proboscis is used to dig burrows although this worm usually leaves its head out at one end, alert for food, and its anus the other, to deposit piles of fecal material. The longest species reach lengths of about 2.5 m (8 ft), with the average being about 45 cm (18 in).

Peanut worms

Sipunculids are often called peanut worms because, when alarmed, they contract their bodies to the shape of a small nut. In fact the group includes a wide variety of species, with perhaps as many as 320 in existence. It is believed that they first arose in the Cambrian Period, and fossils from this period show that they have changed little in the intervening eons. They are distributed across a wide range of habitats, almost all of which are in shallow water. While some make burrows in soft rock, others inhabit empty mollusk shells or crevices in coral reefs. One is known to bore into wood. They average about 10 cm (4 in) in length.

Peanut worms feed in one of two ways. Some use a proboscis armed with a ring of tentacles rooted in the mouth. Food is trapped in the mucus that covers the tentacles, to be drawn into the mouth along the cilia. Otherwise, burrowing peanut worms ingest sand and silt, drawing from it their food.

There are male and female peanut worms but they don't get together for reproduction. Both eggs and sperm are released into the water to be fertilized. The young are born as either larvae or small worms.

Class Pterobranchia

The Pterobranchia class covers about 30 different species of colonial worms that live on the sea bed in tubes made from bodily secretions. They are small creatures that typically do not exceed 5 mm (0.2 in) in length and are usually found in deep water. There they feed on plankton filtered from the surrounding water using specially adapted cilia. They are capable of reproducing sexually after the females lay large numbers of eggs which are fertilized by the males. These hatch into free-swimming larvae which settle on the sea bed where they develop into adults. But they can also reproduce asexually, by budding. Originally they were grouped together with bryozoans and the two share some characteristics.

Priapulids

The mud-dwelling marine worms in the phylum Priapulida fall into three classes: the Priapulimorpha, Halicryptomorpha, and Seticoronaria. The smallest range in length from 5 mm to 200 mm (0.2 to 8 in) and prefer warmer seas. Larger priapulids, which can measure 30 cm (12 in), are happiest in colder waters and can even be found in Antarctica. The 16 known living species are all hermaphroditic, producing

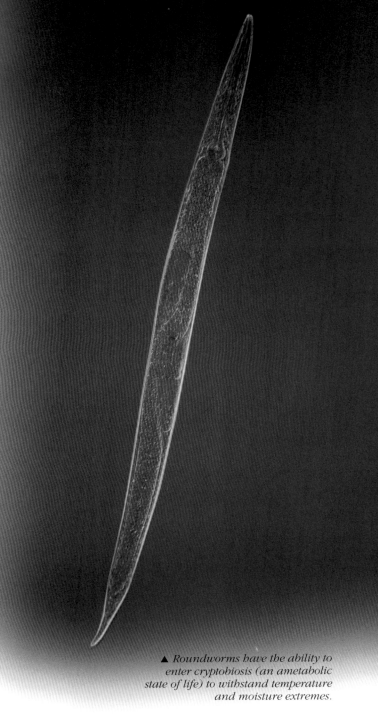

▲ *Roundworms have the ability to enter cryptobiosis (an ametabolic state of life) to withstand temperature and moisture extremes.*

eggs that hatch into free-swimming larvae. As adults, the larger varieties are predators, feeding on more or less any other invertebrates that they can find and overpower. Smaller types are believed to make a meal of bacteria. The phylum is represented in the fossil record from the Middle Cambrian Period onwards.

Brachiopods

Brachiopods make up a large phylum of mostly extinct hard-shelled marine worms. About 100 genera are in existence today but about 12,000 further species have been identified from the fossil record. There are two basic types of brachiopod: those with articulated shells and those where there are no hinges. The latter were the first to evolve, probably arising in the early Cambrian Period. The living representatives of these in the genus Lingula have changed little in 500 million years. Most brachiopods attach themselves to a fixed substrate using a long stalk. This raises them high enough to avoid the risk of becoming silted-over.

Mud dragons

The phylum Kinorhyncha comprises two orders of small marine creatures that are sometimes referred to as 'mud dragons'. They are typically less than 1 mm (0.04 in) in length, and live in soft mud or sand where they feed on organic matter. They can be found anywhere from the coastal shallows to the deepest reaches. Although they are sufficiently evolved to have a distinct head and neck and bodies with eleven segments, they lack any kind of limbs. To move around they push the front part of the body in the desired direction, and then grip the substrate with a series of spines. The rear of the body is then pulled forwards.

Water bears

Hardy Tardigrades are minute segmented creatures with eight legs that are found in a variety of mostly moist environments ranging from the tops of mountains to the abyssal deep. They are remarkable for being able to survive the very harshest conditions. Some species can cope with temperatures from close to absolute zero up to highs of around 150°C (302°F). They are sometimes referred to as 'water bears' because of the manner in which they walk. Although some are predators, most feed on plant matter or bacteria and range in length from 0.3 to 0.5 mm (0.01–0.02 in).

Symbions

The phylum Cycliophora contains a single genus of small recently-discovered creatures known as 'Symbions'. These have sac-like bodies and live on the mouthparts of cold water lobsters, including the Norway, American, and European lobsters. They feed on any edible material left over after the host animal has finished eating. There are three stages in the life cycle, and they can reproduce both sexually and asexually.

Gastrotricha

Microscopic creatures from the phylum Gastrotricha live in both fresh water and marine environments and are often found in profusion in tidal zones. They resemble flatworms in appearance, with flattened transparent bodies and a bilateral symmetry. Adults grow to lengths of up to 3 mm (0.12 in) which, on a diet of tiny dead or living organic particles is no mean feat. There are no dedicated organs for respiration or circulation and all individuals are hermaphroditic. The marine species are mostly found living in the gaps between solid particles on the sea bed.

◀ *Most brachiopods avoid picking locations where they would be subject to strong currents or waves.*

▶ *A magnified image of a water bear; this animal is less than one mm in length.*

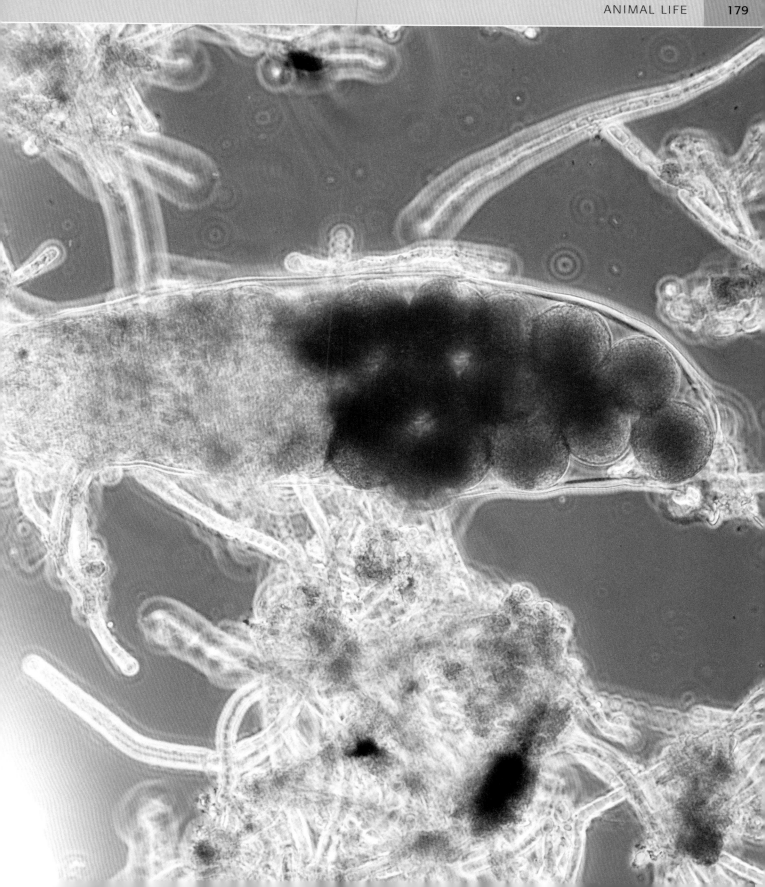

Ribbon worms

Ribbon worms grow to various lengths but are mostly distinctive for their color schemes, which can be bright and patterned.

The phylum Nemertea, to which they belong, is comprised of two classes divided across 250 different genera. Although some of the group live on land or in fresh water, most of the 1,400 or so known species are marine, being found in all of the world's seas and oceans.

They all have thin unsegmented bodies and a powerful proboscis protrudes where the head should be. There are no respiratory organs, with all gaseous exchanges being achieved by diffusion through the skin. The nervous system is well defined, with a distinct brain and nerve cords. Most species can have between two and six eyes, although some have hundreds of light-sensitive cells. There is no heart, but there is a fully functional circulatory system, complete with special structures that act as an effective excretory mechanism.

Typically they live on or under the surface of the sea bed, usually taking advantage of any suitable cover by hiding themselves amongst rocks, seaweed, gravel beds or in soft mud. While a few are scavengers or feed on plant matter, the majority are predators, killing various kinds of invertebrate, including crustaceans and other marine worms. In some species of ribbon worm, the prey is hunted down and attacked with a specially adapted proboscis extension called a stylet. This is used to repeatedly stab the victim and, in some species,

◄ *Nemerteans or proboscis worms and sea stars feed on seal feces underneath a Weddell seal breathing hole in Antarctica.*

poison them too. Other members of the group which lack the stylet use special glue-like secretions to entrap their victims. Once the victim is made helpless it is either swallowed whole or has its tissues sucked out.

The Nemerteans know more size variation than any other kind of animal. The smallest examples may only be a modest 5 mm (0.2 in) long. However, the largest specimens of the European species *Lineus longissimus* reach lengths of at least 30 m (100 ft). There are unsubstantiated reports of examples as long as 60 m (200 ft), which would make it the longest creature in the animal kingdom.

Most of the marine species have separate sexes with fertilization taking place externally and the resultant offspring being laid as eggs. The eggs usually hatch into small versions of the adults, but in some there is an intermediary larval form. A few of the species, however, have internal fertilization and several give birth to live young. This diverse range of physiological adaptations in what are relatively primitive creatures suggests that the Nemertean worms have been in existence for a considerable time. Probably they first evolved relatively early, as far back as the Cambrian Period. However, being soft-bodied, they are almost absent from the fossil record. This makes it extremely difficult to determine their ancestral history. This is not helped by the complexity of the relationships between the various species in the phylum, and as a result there is considerable taxonomic confusion.

▼ *In most species of ribbon worm, the zygote develops into a ciliated, helmet-shaped larval form called pilidium.*

Platyhelminthes

Flatworms, tapeworms and flukes all belong to the same biological group called Platyhelminthes. All have simple, unsegmented bodies, ideal for the parasites. One type, the Monogenea, for example, lives on the outsides of its hosts while the others – the Cestoda (tapeworms) and the Trematoda (flukes) – are internal parasites. The Turbellaria, which are all those worms that are not parasitic, do not depend on a host and are abundant in number.

Some of the marine members of this class use aposematic, bright body coloration, seen as an advertising signal to warn other animals that they are toxic.

There are over 1,000 members of the class Cestoda , best known for infesting land animals. However, some, such as those in the genus *Diphyllobothrium*, live in the digestive tracts of fish. One of the main species – *Diphyllobothrium latum* – is often referred to as the 'fish tapeworm' or 'broad fish tapeworm'. Another well-known example is *Diphyllobothrium dendriticum*, the salmon tapeworm.

Both the cestodes and the trematodes undergo a complex life cycle. In tapeworms this starts when the hermaphroditic adult releases a body segment called a proglottid into the gut of the host. This contains the eggs, which are then released

▼ *Flatworms are often mistaken for sea slugs because of their brilliant colorful patterns.*

into the wider environment as part of the host's excretion. In aquatic or marine environments, these then float in the water until they are eaten by other creatures. In the case of the fish tapeworm, if the cycle is to successfully continue, this has to be a small crustacean, such as a copepod. At this point, the eggs hatch into what are referred to as 'procercoid larvae'. If the intermediary host, the crustacean, is then eaten by a larger animal, such as a fish, the tapeworm larvae then burrow their way out of the gut into the muscles of the new host. There, they develop into a new larval form called a 'plerocercoid larva'. Should this host be eaten by a larger predator, the larvae then begin developing into adults in the small intestine, and the cycle repeats itself.

The process is much the same for the trematodes, except that the eggs are directly released by the adult without recourse to a proglottid stage.

The members of the monogean class live either on the skin or in the gills of a wide variety of fish species, attaching themselves using various kinds of hooks.

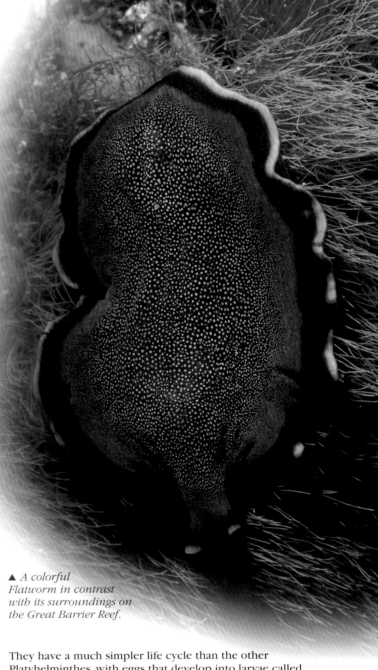

▲ *A colorful Flatworm in contrast with its surroundings on the Great Barrier Reef.*

They have a much simpler life cycle than the other Platyhelminthes, with eggs that develop into larvae called 'oncomiracidium'. These then gradually develop into adults.

All members of the phylum share a number of common physiological characteristics. These include the lack of a body cavity and any kind of respiratory or circulatory organs. They rely on gas diffusion to obtain sufficient oxygen and, as a result of this, they are unable to develop deep body tissues which is why they are flat.

Annelids

The phylum Annelida is made up of
several classes of different ringed
worms. These include the Hirudinea
(leeches, of which some are marine),
the Myzostomida (small parasitic
worms that live on crinoids) and the
Haplodrili, or Archiannelida (primitive
marine worms). However, even with
their numbers combined, they are far
outnumbered by the polychaete worms

The true worms or 'polychaetes', are
segmented marine worms that inhabit almost
all of the world's oceanic environments. It is
probable that they first evolved in the Cambrian
Period, around 450 million years ago. The class
contains around 9,000 different species, with
these being divided into about 80 families. It is no
easy task to draw a distinction between them either.
Many can only be differentiated through microscopic
examination. One big difference that's apparent more
immediately is that some are errant or free moving
while others are sedentary, which means they stay in
one place.

Some of the more commonly recognized species
include ragworms (also called the sandworm or clam
worm), lugworms, bristleworms and featherduster
worms. The smallest of the true worms measure less
than 1 mm (0.04 in) long, while some of the larger
ones, such as Eunice gigantea, can grow to lengths
of as much as 3 m (10 ft).

All true worms have characteristic fleshy
structures called parapodia. These carry a
number of chitinous bristles called chaetae.

Polychaetes, especially those rooted to
one spot, can be filter feeders or detritus
eaters. The rest that move are scavengers
and nocturnal predators, with jaws
and teeth. When they have eaten the
food goes into a digestive tract that
stretches from nose to tail. Sand is
usually among the waste material
deposited by the worms on the sea
bed in the form of casts. Others are
parasites of larger marine creatures.
In some habitats, their population
densities can be extraordinarily
high. This is especially true in
places like estuary mud, where
they can teem in unimaginable

◄ *Fan worms, also known as feather
duster worms, are found in nearly all
tropical regions of the world.*

numbers. As a result of this, they form a vital link in a locality's food chain and are often a major food source for many larger marine creatures, such as crabs, fish and birds.

Their lifestyles vary tremendously, from those which float freely to those that burrow into the sea bed at great depths. Some of the burrowers live in holes that they form in thick mud as they dig, whereas others construct tubes which project out the sea bed. There are many species which do not make any kind of shelter at all but bury themselves under rocks or in gravel beds.

Although polychaetes dominate in terms of numbers there are other notable annelids. The Pompeii worm (*Alvinella pompejana*), discovered fairly recently, is remarkable for its ability to live in close proximity to the excessive temperatures of the hydrothermal vents found in the depths of the Pacific Ocean.

The beard worms, which belong to the family Siboglinidae, were previously classified as Pogonophora (the giant tube worms) and Vestimentifera. Although they can be quite long – up to 2.5 m (8 ft) in length, they are typically very thin.

There are three orders of Echiura, or spoon worms. These have multiple stages in their life cycles, beginning with an egg, which is followed by a free-swimming larval form. After this they either grow directly into an adult, or pass through an intermediate stage. Spoon worms mostly inhabit sand burrows and mud or live in gaps amongst rocks, gravel beds or coral reefs. They are distributed from the coastal shallows right down into the abyssal depths, with most feeding by capturing suspended particles from the surrounding water.

▼ *The feather duster worm feeds on plankton caught with its feathery gills*

PLANKTON

The multitude of microscopic plants and animals that floats with the winds and currents on or near the ocean's surface is collectively known as plankton. Most are simple, rounded, single-cell organisms, but don't let their miniscule size lead you to think they are unimportant. As the foundation of the food chain, there's little to top them in terms of significance.

There are two types; phytoplankton, composed of microscopic plants and bacteria, and zooplankton, composed of microscopic animals. Both are also important indicators of environmental and marine health.

Phytoplankton live in the sunlit zone and rely on light and nutrients for growth. They are very sensitive to changes of temperature and differing levels of food. Inside their simple structures, they contain the pigment chlorophyll used for photosynthesis, the process in which water molecules and atmospheric carbon dioxide are fused into carbohydrates to make plant food. It is chlorophyll that gives phytoplankton its greenish tinge. In ideal conditions phytoplankton grow so rapidly and in such numbers that they 'bloom' across the surface of the ocean and become visible to the naked eye.

An individual phytoplankter lives for a day or two at most. When it dies it sinks to the ocean floor to join the plant and animal material already lodged there. In this way, over millennia, the ocean bed has become the largest storage sink for atmospheric carbon dioxide – an estimated 90 per cent of it is down there.

▼ *Antarctic krill schooling underwater; this small shrimp-like crustacean is the most important zooplankton in the Antarctic food web.*

Among the many types of zooplankton are numerous micro-scopic animals as well as the larval and youthful stages of fish, or invertebrates like jellyfish, squid and snails.

Zooplankton live in the sunlit zone as well as the deeper reaches of the ocean and are, like their plant cousins, important indicators of water quality. To survive, zooplankton must eat other plankton and are themselves a vital food source for the larval stages of many kinds of fish as well as a nutritious food stuff for foraging fish species. High levels of zooplankton indicate healthy fish populations.

Ascending the evolutionary ladder, krill are small, pink, shrimp-like crustaceans and comprise about 84 different species, many of them region-specific. They live in vast swarms in the sunlit and twilight zones of the world's oceans and can be anything from 7 mm (0.3 in) to 5 cm (2 in) long. Some even produce their own bioluminescence.

In tropical waters krill eat phytoplankton. Some species also eat zooplankton. They can develop in such vast numbers that dense 'clouds' of krill cover the waters producing a feeding bonanza for other species, especially whales, fish, seals, penguins, mantas, squid and some ocean-going birds. They are a vital food source for many creatures and when krill numbers decline other higher life forms noticeably suffer.

During daylight krill congregate at depths of around 100 m (328 ft), although some species dive much deeper. Then, at night, they swim up to the ocean surface. Such diurnal migration helps them to conserve energy and avoid predators. Although they are able to swim, krill are nonetheless at the mercy of currents and winds.

Krill are swimming crustaceans with a segmented body, a hard exoskeleton and numerous legs. In warm waters on summer nights the females lay up to 1,000 eggs that gently drift down to the ocean depths where many are eaten by fish and other creatures. The relatively few eggs that survive hatch into young krill that rise to the surface, where they are often classified as zooplankton. As the young krill grow they discard their exoskeleton and grow a new covering.

▶ *Different species of phytoplankton come in many different shapes and sizes. but they all get their green color from chlorophyll.*

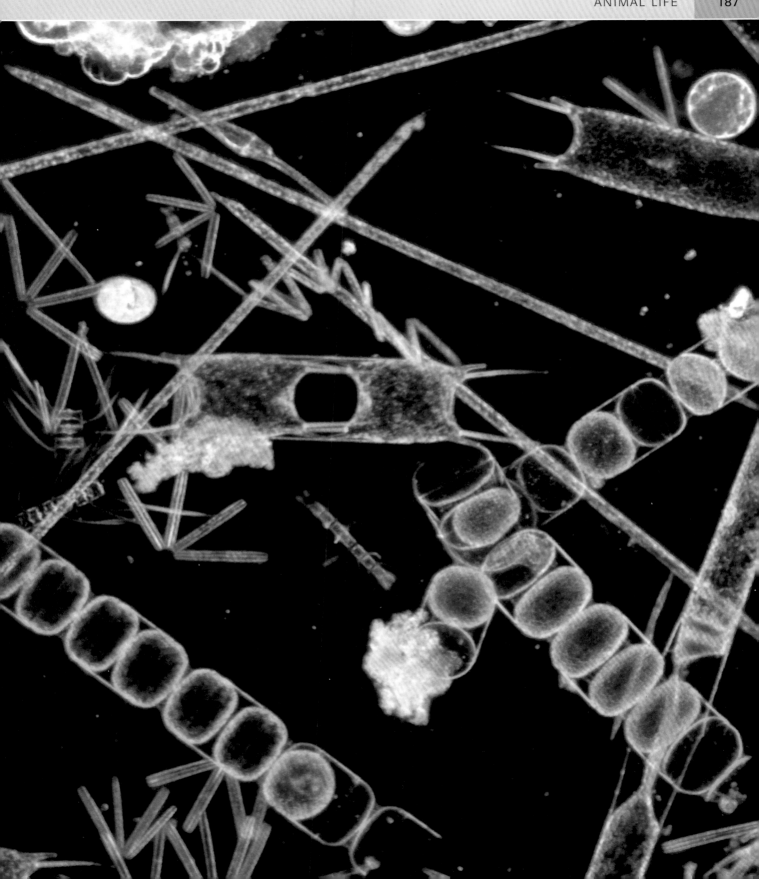

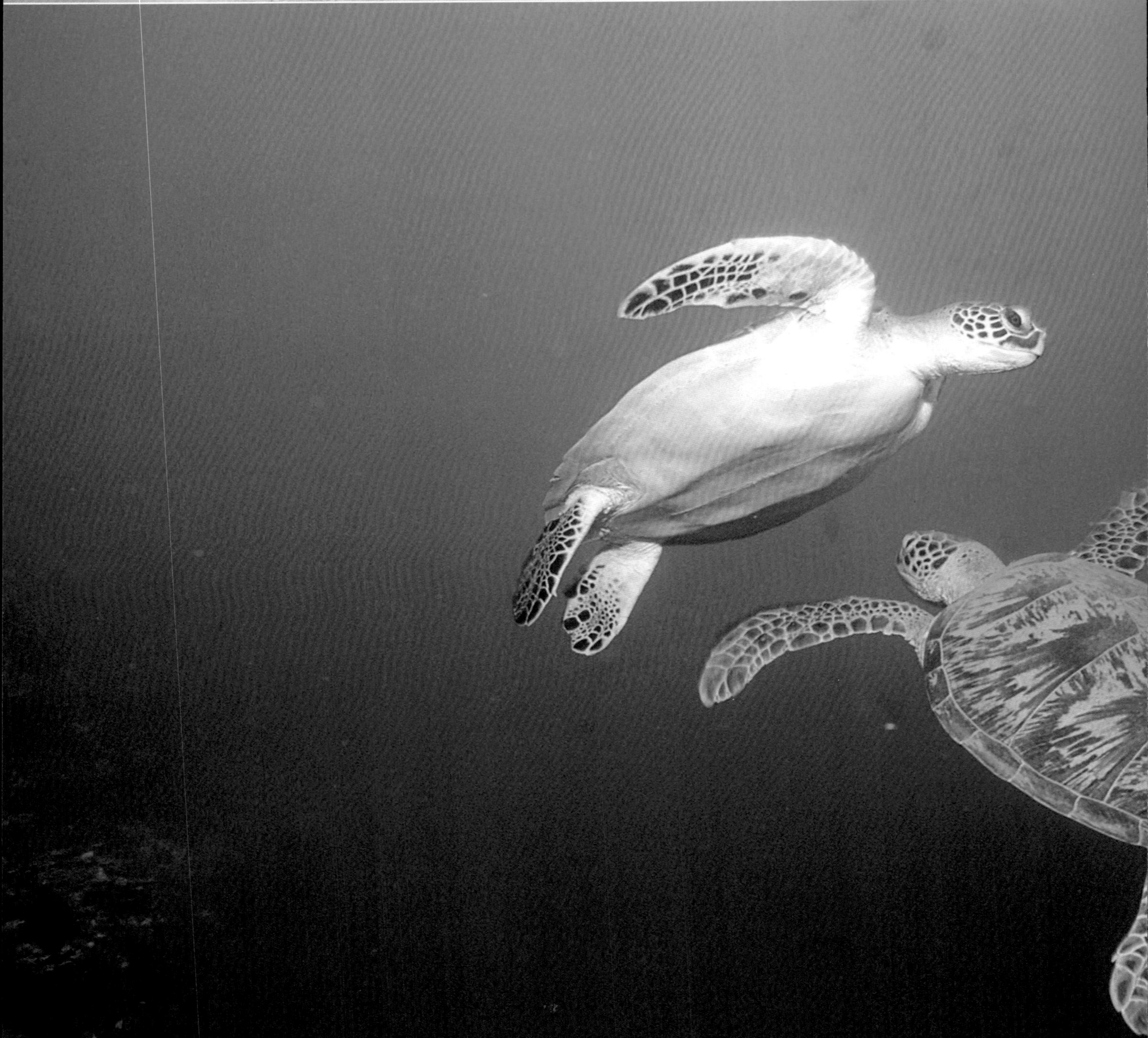

REPTILES

There are comparatively few reptiles who call the world's oceans home. These include the American and the saltwater crocodiles, the marine iguana, seven species of sea turtle, and just over 60 species of sea snake.

This was not always the case, though. Back in the age of the dinosaur, the seas were populated by all manner of reptilians. The first evolved during the Permian period, which began some 300 million years ago. As time went on, they grew bigger, with one of the better known orders being the ichthyosaurs – the 'fish lizards' – which lived from about 245 million years ago to about 90 million years ago. They were eventually displaced by the plesiosaurs, easily recognizable with their broad bodies, long necks, short tails and flipper limbs. For many millions of years, these spectacular creatures, along with giant sharks, more or less dominated the oceans. Like many other animals on the planet, however, they all died out around 65 million years ago. With the exception of most sea snakes, today's marine reptiles are still dependent on the land, having to return to solid ground to lay their eggs.

◀ *Turtles – such as these green sea turtles – are believed to have inhabited the oceans for around 250 million years.*

Crocodiles

▼ This saltwater crocodile is pictured off the Queensland coast of Australia.

Although the American and saltwater crocodiles do live in the sea, they are not creatures of the open oceans. The American crocodile is mostly found on the coasts of Central America. These include the waters of both the Atlantic and Pacific, and range from Peru in the south to Florida in the north as well as parts of the Caribbean. They can reach around 6 m (20 ft) in length.

The saltwater crocodile is larger still, with some individuals reputedly reaching as much as 8 or 9 m (26–30 ft) in length and some 1,300 kg (2,900 lb) in weight. This makes it the world's largest living reptile. As a result of hunting by humans, it is no longer found in many of its former territories, including Thailand, Laos and Vietnam. These days it is only found along the coasts of some areas of southern Asia eastwards from India and down through Indonesia as far as Australia. Although it is not a true open ocean species, there are accounts of individuals appearing well away from their usual ranges, having swum vast distances to do so.

Lizards

Somewhat surprisingly, considering the number of different lizard species that occur across the world, the only representative of this numerous group to live in the sea is the Galápagos marine iguana (*Amblyrhynchus cristatus*). As its common name would suggest, it is only found on the Galápagos Islands off the Pacific coast of South America. Like the crocodiles, however, it is not an open ocean species, living among the rocks, marshes and mangroves of the coastal fringes of its home territories. It is a dark colored creature that grows to about 1.7 m (5.6 ft) in length, and feeds on seaweed and marine algae, browsing at depths of up to 10 m (33 ft) or more. It has evolved into an excellent swimmer, having a flattened tail which allows it to cope with the harsh currents that are characteristic of its home environment. It also has sharp claws that enable it to hold onto the rocks even when they are washed over by powerful waves. It is not so well suited to being out of the water, however, and makes awkward progress on land.

▼ *A marine iguana returns to the surface after feasting on seaweed in the wave-washed shallows of Santa Cruz Island.*

for example, are known to swim to depths of around 1,190 m (3,900 ft) while hunting. This is because they have a slow metabolism, very high levels of red blood cells and an ingenious mechanism that diverts oxygen-rich blood away from low priority tissues to the heart, brain and nervous system.

Sea turtles have also evolved an efficient method of expelling salt from their bodies, via special tear ducts known as lacrimal glands. Depending on the species concerned, these are situated in the corners of the eyes, in the nostril, or on the tongue.

Although members of this group spend the majority of their lives at sea, their terrestrial ancestry means that females have to return to land to lay eggs. This is a hazardous time as, once out of the water, turtles are poorly equipped for speed and are therefore vulnerable to attack. The eggs – typically between 50 and 200 – are laid in shallow pits on sandy beaches. These holes are then filled in and abandoned. Now it is the eggs that are at risk, susceptible to the vagaries of the weather and any local predators which may include anything from dingoes through lizards to humans. Each turtle then returns to the oceans until the next time she is due to lay eggs. Once mature, this happens every two to four years. Male turtles almost never leave the water.

▲ *A hawksbill turtle indulges in a meal of fresh jellyfish.*

Sea turtles

Unlike crocodiles and lizards, sea turtles are truly at home in the open ocean; there are seven species of sea turtle alive today. These are the flatback turtle, green sea turtle, hawksbill turtle, Kemp's Ridley sea turtle, leatherback sea turtle, loggerhead sea turtle and the Olive Ridley sea turtle.

It is thought that sea turtles first evolved from land-based ancestors between 250 and 220 million years ago. During this time, they have become superbly well adapted to life in the sea. They have powerful paddle-like forelimbs which make them strong swimmers. This is a vital feature for creatures that inhabit the wild oceans. They are also able to dive to great depths in search of their prey which mostly consists of jellyfish. Consequently discarded carrier bags, that can resemble jellyfish, pose a threat to turtles. In spite of the fact that they are air breathers, they can stay submerged for extended periods. Leatherbacks,

▶ *A pair of green sea turtles mating off the coast of East Borneo.*

▲ *Green sea turtles can
live to the ripe old age of
80 years old in the wild.*

The hatchlings emerge from their eggs at night about two
months later, whereupon they have to make the most
treacherous journey of their lives. This involves burrowing
up to the surface of the sand then trying to make it into the
sea before dawn. In daylight they are at risk from many kinds
of predators, with attacks by gulls and frigate birds being
particularly prevalent, and may dry out in the sun. Streetlights
and car headlights help to confuse young turtles who are
guided to the water's edge by the reflection of moonlight
on the sea. In the water they still have to avoid the perils of
marauding fish – especially sharks. Only a small percentage of
young turtles make it to the relative safety of the open ocean.
It takes them many years – usually decades – before they reach
sexual maturity and they may live around 80 years in total.

Flatback turtle

Distinctive for laying larger but fewer eggs than the rest, the
flatback turtle (*Natator depressus*) is an Australasian species
known for the shape of its shell. Living relatively close to the
shore, flatback turtles inhabit the shallow waters of estuaries,
reefs and lagoons. They range from Indonesia southwards to
the northern coast of Australia, where they feed on a wide
variety of foodstuffs including fish, small crustaceans, jellyfish,
soft coral, mollusks and seaweed. They may grow to lengths
of around 90 cm (35 inches), and are considered at risk of
extinction.

Green sea turtle

The green sea turtle (*Chelonia mydas*) is not named after its
overall color which varies widely but for the layers of green
fat found under its shell. It lives in shallow waters throughout
the warmer parts of the Atlantic, Indian and Pacific Oceans
where it has a mostly herbivorous diet, feeding on various
kinds of seagrass. On average it grows to around 1.5m (5 ft)
in length and about 200 kg (440 lb) in weight, although much
larger individuals have been recorded. A powerful swimmer,
it migrates over long distances to reach its breeding grounds.
Again, it is an endangered species that is protected in most
countries.

▲ *An Olive Ridley sea turtle swims near the surface around the Galapagos Islands.*

Kemp's Ridley sea turtle

The rarest of all sea turtles is the Kemp's Ridley sea turtle (*Lepidochelys kempii*). It grows to around 95 cm (3 ft) in length and about 45 kg (100 lb) in weight, and is found in the warm and temperate waters of the Atlantic Ocean and the Gulf of Mexico. Its diet consists of seaweed, algae, certain crustaceans, jellyfish, sea urchins and mollusks. Although they are endangered, they are still hunted in Mexico for food and as a source of leather. They are also threatened by pollution, habitat loss and by fishing operations, when they become part of the secondary catch.

Olive Ridley sea turtle

Smallest of all the sea turtles, the Olive Ridley or Pacific Ridley sea turtle (*Lepidochelys olivacea*) is also generally considered to be the commonest species too. Its population has, however, fallen dramatically in recent years as the result of human encroachment and it is currently listed as vulnerable. It only grows to around 70 cm (28 in) in length and about 40 kg (88 lb) in weight. It is found in the tropical and warmer temperate waters around the world and, although it does frequent the open ocean, it is mostly found within about 16 km (10 miles) of the coast. Its diet is similar to that of its nearest relation, Kemp's Ridley sea turtle.

Leatherback sea turtle

The leatherback sea turtle (*Dermochelys coriacea*) is so named because unlike other sea turtles, it does not have a hard carapace. Instead, it is covered by a leathery skin. It is easily the largest of the group, with average body lengths of up to 2 m (6.6 ft) and a weight of around 700 kg (1,543 lb). Much bigger examples have been recorded, however. It has particularly long front flippers which can reach 2.7 m (8.9 ft) in length. These help it to swim at great speed and it can achieve up to 35 kph (22 mph). Consequently it is capable of covering vast distances. It is distributed throughout most of the world's seas and oceans, with the exception of the cold waters of the polar regions. The species is able to dive to great depths – at least 1200 m (3937 ft) – where it hunts for jellyfish.

Loggerhead sea turtle

The loggerhead sea turtle (*Caretta caretta*) is found in tropical and temperate waters of the Atlantic, Indian and Pacific Oceans, as well as the Mediterranean Sea. It feeds on jellyfish, various kinds of eggs, a wide variety of crustaceans and mollusks, as well as any fish it can catch. It does not reach sexual maturity until it is about 35 years old, by which time it will have reached between 80 and 120 cm (2.6–4 ft) in length and an average weight of about 115 kg (254 lb). The species is considered endangered, with the main threats being from Man and via the ravaging of hatchlings by racoons and other carnivores. Despite being given international protection, both the flesh and eggs are still eaten by humans in countries such as Mexico.

▲ *A leatherback turtle hatchling takes to the water; this is the most dangerous time for youngsters and only a minority reach maturity.*

▼ *A loggerhead sea turtle at Gray's Reef National Marine Sanctuary, one of the largest near-shore 'live-bottom' reefs of the southeastern United States.*

Sea Snakes

The sea snakes are a large but little understood group of animals that evolved from terrestrial snakes. Their exact taxonomic status has been confused over the years, and the complexity of the relationships between them means the situation still remains unclear today. The simplest arrangement puts 57 species into 16 genera of true sea snakes, and 5 into one genus of sea kraits.

Most sea snakes are comparatively small, only growing to about 1.5 m (5 ft) long. However, some species can reach around 3 m (10 ft) in length. The majority have become so specialized for their marine environments that they have completely lost the ability to move on dry land. This is due to the loss of the scales that allow them to grip the ground and therefore achieve forward motion. The only exception is the sea kraits, which can still move around, although not nearly as well as their land-dwelling cousins. This is not the problem that it initially appears, as – apart from the five species of sea kraits – they have evolved to deliver live young underwater. As a result, they do not have to make landfall to lay eggs. Another adaptation for a marine existence can be seen in the tail which has developed into a flattened paddle-like structure to help them to swim more easily.

Although they have evolved to move well in water, sea snakes still have to breathe fresh air as they do not have gills. This means that they have to surface regularly or they will drown. They are, however, able to get a proportion of the oxygen they need directly from the water through respiration via the skin. Thanks to this, it is possible for them to stay underwater for extended periods – up to several hours, if necessary – at depths of up to 90 m (295 ft). They are helped by a lung with a much larger capacity than that found in terrestrial snakes which runs for most of the body length.

All marine animals that evolved from land ancestors have to deal with the ingestion of the large amounts of salt contained in sea water. Without an effective means to control this, most creatures would quickly die. Sea snakes are unusual in that they expel excess salt from specialized structures called the posterior sublingual glands, which are located near the tongue. When the tongue (which is shorter than those of land snakes) moves, salt is discharged from the glands back into the water.

Sea snakes feed on live prey. Accordingly, many have very powerful venom. In spite of this, few humans are killed by these creatures as most are not aggressive unless they are

▼ *A yellow-lipped sea krait off the Indonesian coast. This species can grow up to 3 m (10 ft) in length.*

provoked. The usual symptoms of a bite in a human include varying forms of paralysis. If this spreads to the muscles used in breathing, it can be fatal. The typical diet of a sea snake is fish with eels being a particular favorite. Some species, however, specialize in hunting crustaceans, mollusks or other marine organisms. They mostly hunt using smell detected by special receptors in the tongue. As a result they do not need particularly good vision so their eyes are quite small. It is thought they hunt both by day and night.

Sea snakes live in warm coastal waters and are found in the tropical regions of the Indian and Pacific Oceans, but not the Atlantic. Their habitat ranges from the coast of East Africa to New Zealand and as far as western South America. Northwards, it is from the Gulf of California down to Peru in the Americas and from the Horn of Africa to Cape Town. They are relatively common, with only one species being considered vulnerable

▶ *A pair of banded sea krait engage in mating courtship.*

SPONGES

Sponges are among the most primitive and ancient creatures in the oceans. They evolved over 500 million years ago and have developed into more than 5,000 different species, in the Porifera classification. And it is beyond doubt that there are countless more awaiting discovery. The tropical reef sponges belong to the Scleropongiae or coralline sponges and are broadly classified by their shape. They grow in all three of the primary coral reef zones.

Uniquely among marine invertebrates sponges have a body made entirely of simple cells which are connected by chambers and channels but lack true tissues or organs. Even though they are animals, sponges are so primitive they lack any kind of muscular, circulatory, digestive or nervous system and in the adult form are completely sessile, meaning they do not move location.

▼ *Elephant ear sponge, like this specimen off the Philippines, can grow to 1.8 m (6 ft) across.*

Sponges grow into a huge variety of shapes – cups, tubes, cones, balls, barrels, fans and more – and have a range of colors. Sometimes their appearance changes with their environment which can make identification difficult. They also range in size from a few centimeters across to over 1.8 m (6 ft) in diameter. On reefs many of the coral sponges superficially resemble corals.

The larger sponges pump and filter a colossal volume of water through their bodies. Indeed, sponges are filter feeders, eating plankton and tiny floating organisms drawn in with the water that comes through an external skin made up of thousands of tiny pores (ostia). Under this lies a layer of gel that contains either supportive needles made of calcium carbonate (spicules) or sponging fibres which provide a flexible, protein-based skeleton and give the sponge its shape. One calculation has the sponges in the Caribbean collectively filtering nearly the equivalent volume of the Caribbean Sea every day.

Internally the sponge consists of numerous canals and channels that lead eventually to the central body cavity. Oxygen and nutrients are filtered out and the depleted water ejected at speed through a small aperture called the osculum, along with any waste matter.

Most sponges possess male or female qualities and release sperm or fertilize an egg as required. The embryo becomes a free-swimming microscopic larva that will eventually settle on the seabed and grow into an adult. Many sponges also reproduce asexually by budding when a fragment of body is broken off by water currents and carried to another location where it will grow as a clone of its parent.

▶ *In deeper waters, yellow tube sponges develop long, straight tubes while at shallower depths they resemble a cactus.*

There are many different types of reef sponge and one of the most common is the tube sponge (*Callyspongia vaginalis*). This grows a group of long tubular structures that eject filtered water out through large openings at the top. The vase sponge (*Ircinia campana*) resembles a large inverted bell up to 20 cm (8 in) wide and 90 cm (35 in) wide. It lives attached to rocks in Caribbean waters, as does the red tree sponge (*Haliclona compressa*), a bright red sponge that looks like branch coral but is only about 20 cm (8 in) high. Elsewhere in the Pacific the yellow sponge (*Cleona celata*) grows on the coral reef face.

TUNICATES AND LANCELETS

Tunicates and lancelets are two groups of invertebrates that possess a notochord – a primitive rod-shaped flexible backbone analogous to the vertebral column found in vertebrates.

Tunicates, or urochordates, are a group of sac-like filter feeders that evolved about 540 million years ago and total about 3,000 species, the best known being the sea squirts.

Most tunicates live attached to rocks on the seabed where they filter mighty volumes of water and eat plankton from it through their barrel-shaped, jelly-like bodies. Water is drawn in through one siphon and expelled through another. Internally they contain a large sieve-like structure called a pharynx that traps plankton as seawater is sucked through the body. Other tunicates, like salps and pyrosomes, remain in the open sea, drifting alongside plankton and sometimes congregating in vast swarms.

Hermaphrodite tunicates have eggs in their bodies that are fertilized by free-floating sperm introduced during filter feeding. The fertilized eggs hatch into larvae resembling small tadpoles. After a short swim, they cement themselves to an appropriate surface and metamorphose into the adult form, at which point they lose the notochord. Their sac-shaped bodies are covered with a tough layer of cellulose (they are the only animals able to produce cellulose) called a tunic that also has root-like projections for attaching to rocks.

Lancelets constitute a family of about 25 species, most of them belonging to the *Brachiostoma* genus, living buried in the sediment of shallow temperate and tropical seas. They are thought to be similar to the earliest forms of vertebrates, from which they split over 520 million years ago. Lancelets

▶ *Lancelets are often described as the most primitive fish still in existence today.*

◀ *Blue sea squirts and yellow cave coral combine to create a rainbow of color.*

belong to the sub-phylum Cephalochordata, animals that retain the notochord throughout their life.

These diminutive creatures grow to a maximum of 7 cm (2.8 in). Their body resembles a transparent fish, tapered at both ends, but without fins and with only a notional tail. They have no true skeleton, only some cartilage-like material around the mouth, tail and gill slits. Lacking eyes and complex sense organs, or even a true brain, their colorless blood has no hemoglobin and they breathe through their skin. Their body is composed of a series of overlapping chevron-shaped blocks of muscles, called myomeres, which the animal flexes to swim. The dorsal nerve chord is protected by a notochord.

Their principal sensory devices are thin, stiff, tentacle-like strands hanging from the mouth (oral cirri) that also filter their food. Food and water enters through the mouth and is filtered out by the pharynx and expelled through the atriopore. In order to take on board water they anchor themselves in the sand using what passes as a tail.

Male and female lancelets release sperm and eggs into the water in the hope they will unite. The fertilized eggs hatch into a larva that closely resembles the adult but lives in the sunlit zone. There they eat a diet of plankton until metamorphosis into the adult stage at which time they descend to live on the sea floor.

They are strong swimmers but live most of their lives buried in sand or sediment with only their mouths projecting into the water. In parts of Asia they are commercially harvested.

Coral Reefs

Live coral is essentially a community of tiny animals, each encased in a protective 'cup' of calcium carbonate crystals, or corallite, produced from the lower part of their stalk. The reefs formed by these creatures are among the natural world's greatest wonders; beautiful, colorful, complex, sometimes huge structures, throbbing with ocean life of all kinds.

▲ The Great Barrier Reef, the largest reef in the world.

CORAL REEFS

Coral reefs support more species than any other marine environment and there are undoubtedly many more to be discovered judging by an intensive study of the fossil record on the Paleobiology Database (a collaborative project organized by researchers around the world). Scientists discovered that new species originate 50 per cent faster in a coral reef ecosystem compared to other habitats, making them evolutionary hotspots and incredibly valuable ecologically.

Most are found in the tropical waters of the Pacific (especially the western Pacific) and Indian Oceans and, although occupying less than one per cent of the ocean surface, house at least 25 per cent of all marine species. It is worth pointing out that reefs are formed from 'stony', or calcium-producing corals, which make up most coral species. 'Soft' corals play no part in the process although both types are members of a cnidarian group known as the Class Anthozoa.

Formation of reefs

Coral reefs are usually found in the warm, shallow waters of the sunlit zone where a regular, gentle wave action combines with a nutrient-poor, clear water. Consequently, the majority of known reefs occur in tropical and sub-tropical waters between 30°N and 30°S of the equator in waters averaging between 26 and 27°C (78.8–80°F).

The highest concentrations of these reefs lie between the Red Sea and the central Pacific Ocean, although there are also lots in the Caribbean. They are absent from areas of upwelling, cold coastal currents or where huge fresh water outflows from large river systems dilute the waters.

Almost all coral reefs in the world are less than 10,000 years old. This is because they formed after the last glacial period when the melting ice raised sea levels around the world and

flooded the continental shelves where reefs subsequently formed. The oldest and biggest reefs expanded upwards, keeping pace with rising sea levels, while those which failed to grow fast enough lost the sunlight and died; these structures are known as drowned reefs.

There are three main types – the fringing reef, barrier reef and atoll reef – plus a further five which have slightly different characteristics: the patch, apron, bank, ribbon and table reef. Most common are fringing reefs, which lie just offshore and more or less parallel to it, separated by only a shallow channel (and sometimes not even that). They are located on the upper continental shelf as upward-growing corals and create an underwater barrier between sea and land. They may alter the shape of the shoreline or form arcs of coral islands.

◀ *The Germans blasted a channel in this Micronesian reef for easier shipping access in the 1900s.*

▶ *Coral reefs tend to be a colorful feature of the oceans and are teeming with life.*

A barrier reef grows parallel to the coast but much further out – sometimes many kilometers – and is separated from the land by a deep lagoon. These reefs can be huge, tens of meters long, and very deep and wide although they still contain distinct zones of coral growth. The most famous is the Great Barrier Reef off the north-east coast of Queensland, Australia which runs for around 2,000 km (1,243 miles). The second largest is the Belize Barrier Reef which stretches for around 900 km (560 miles) from southern Mexico and along the coast of Belize to the islands of Honduras.

An atoll is a continuous circular barrier reef surrounding an open lagoon. Found mostly in the tropical regions of the Pacific, this type breaks the surface to become a thin, circular island made entirely of disintegrated coral which has been battered by wind and wave action. The vast majority of atolls have their origin in ancient volcanoes and take as long as thirty million years to form. There are two types; those found on the continental shelf and those emerging from deep water.

Atolls typically start as a fringing reef around a volcano, their coral continuing to grow as the volcano gradually subsides. Eventually, after tens of thousands of years, the volcano becomes completely submerged and then disappears altogether, leaving a clear lagoon encircled by coral. Atolls can often be seen clustered in groups – Tuamotu Island, the Marshall Islands, the Maldives, and the Coral Sea Islands are all good examples in the Pacific – while one of the largest is the Great Chagos Bank, in the Chagos Archipelago of the Indian Ocean. This covers an area of 12,642 square kilometers (4,881 square miles) but only about 4.5 square kilometers (1.7 square miles) can accurately be described as land.

There are five 'variants' of coral formation associated with reefs: a ribbon reef is the outer long, narrow, wavy structure, often found around atolls, a patch reef is a stand-alone, usually circular, outcrop common within lagoons while a bank reef is similar to the patch but longer and sometimes semi-circular. Table reefs are effectively patch reefs minus a lagoon, while apron reefs are a shorter, more sloping, version of the fringing reef and stretch outwards and downwards from the shore.

Coral also contributes to the creation of low-level sandy islands, known as cays (or keys), seen in tropical waters across the Indian, Atlantic and Pacific oceans. They are composed of eroded reef material piled above sea level and, when colonized and stabilized by plants, they can become inhabited islands with land suitable for agriculture.

In tropical or equatorial latitudes stony corals (i.e. those which produce the familiar calcium carbonate reef-forming shell) grow in sunlit, nutrient-poor, clear, warm waters up to

▼ *A distinctive coral reef and lagoon, Marshall Islands, Ailinglaplap Atoll, Micronesia.*

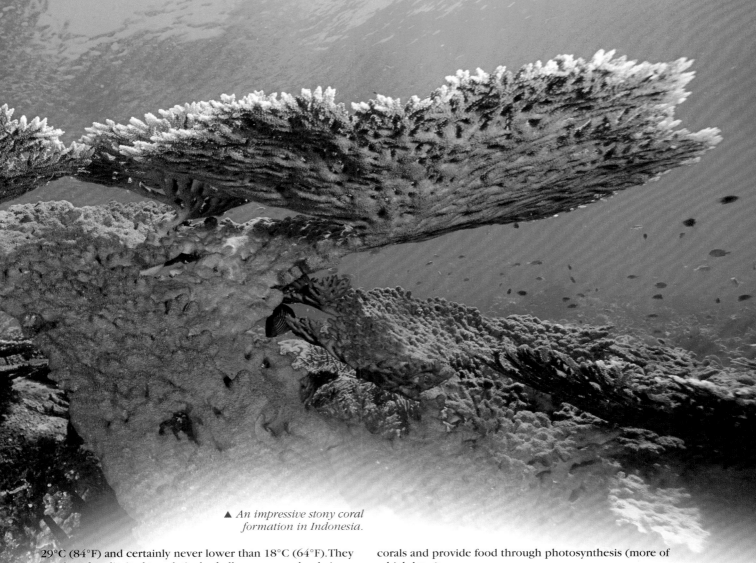

▲ *An impressive stony coral formation in Indonesia.*

29°C (84°F) and certainly never lower than 18°C (64°F). They are therefore limited to relatively shallow areas and only in exceptionally clear sea conditions can they exist as low as 60 m (200 ft). Healthy corals grow horizontally between 1 and 3 cm (0.39-1.2 in) a year and vertically as much as 25 cm (10 in) a year. Where a reef is raised above sea level by underlying tectonic activity, the coral will die and become white limestone.

The fact that corals prefer to grow in water that is poor in nutrients seems like a bit of a paradox: how do coral polyps survive without a constant supply of food from the surrounding water? Scientists may have found a clue in the profusion of small sponges which thrive in nooks and crannies within the reef; it is thought that these sponges consume around 60 per cent of the available plankton, and that the waste they excrete acts as food for the coral. In addition, further nourishment is provided by the symbiotic zooxanthellae algae, which live in the gut tissue of tropical

corals and provide food through photosynthesis (more of which later).

Cold water coral reefs are a relatively recent discovery (1869) and although not as well studied appear to support as rich and diverse an environment as tropical reefs. Most have been found in the North Atlantic, especially off the Norwegian coast and the western coast of Scotland, and this is probably a direct result of seabed surveying for oil. It is likely that many more will be found across the oceans as oil exploration extends ever further and deeper; we already know of some thriving at depths of almost 3,000 m (10,000 ft).

Cold water reefs are not as colorful, large or complex as their tropical relatives but they are, at least in one sense, more robust. They are not dependant on the zooxanthellae. Instead they obtain nutrients by filtering food from the water, allowing stony corals on cold water reefs to grow in total darkness at temperatures of between 4 and 13°C (39-55°F).

◄ *An aerial view of the Great Barrier Reef, the world's biggest single structure made by living organisms.*

The Great Barrier Reef

The Great Barrier Reef lies off the north-east coast of Queensland, Australia and is estimated to be between 6,000 and 8,000 years old. It is both the largest coral reef system in the world and the largest animal-made structure, comprising over 2,900 linked reefs and at least 900 islands scattered across 344,400 square kilometers (132,973 square miles) and extending up to 1,000 m (3,281 ft) off the coast. It supports an astonishing number of creatures including over 1,500 species of fish, 125 of shark, skate and stingray, 30 of whales, dolphins

▼ *Heart Reef is located on Hardy Reef and was only 'discovered' in 1975.*

and porpoise's 17 of sea snake, 5,000 of mollusk, 9 of seahorse, 6 of sea turtle, 215 of bird and 2,195 of plant.

This priceless habitat is protected under legislation passed by the Australian government through the Great Barrier Reef Marine Park and is so extensive that it is a considerable hazard to shipping. Indeed, it was discovered when Captain James Cook's ship *Endeavour* ran aground on what is now called Endeavour Reef in June 1770. He and his crew escaped a watery grave only thanks to their superb seamanship.

The reef began growing on the Australian continental shelf some 20,000 years ago when the sea level was 120 m (394 ft) lower than at present and the land was just a hilly coastal plain. As sea levels rose so the corals grew upwards, initially colonizing around the hills and then growing up the hills as they became islands. In time, even the islands were submerged and the corals covered them to form the reefs we see today.

Habitats in harmony

A coral reef provides one of the planet's most biodiverse habitats, supporting some 4,000 species of fish alone. There are also a variety of seaweeds, sponges, jellyfish, crustaceans, sea anemones (themselves a type of coral), conch, worms, mollusks, starfish, sand dollars, sea urchins, sea snakes and sea turtles, to name but a few species (although the only mammals are visiting whales and dolphins). The nutrients within

▶ *A soft coral colony growing amidst large plates of cabbage coral.*

a reef community are not lost into the open ocean; rather they are passed from organism to organism. So we see phytoplankton nutrients being passed from marine worms, to seaweed, to coralline algae to corals and eventually back again.

In total there are about 1,000 species of reef-building corals, the vast majority of which are found in the tropical waters of the western Pacific. Here there are some 75 per cent more genera, and 85 per cent more species, than in the Atlantic Ocean (even including the Caribbean). In Indonesian waters alone there are 581 of the known reef-building species.

There are numerous types of reef-building corals, properly called hermatypic corals, defined by their shape – fan, thorny, pillar and so on. Each branch or frond of coral is made up of thousands of individual marine organisms, called polyps, living on the outer surface. These tiny soft-bodied creatures protect and house themselves on top of previous coral deposits by creating an exoskeleton of cup-shaped corallite calcium deposits (see above). When the polyp dies the corallite remains and another infinitesimally small contribution is made to the reef's mass.

Polyps cluster together and collectively build up individual corals of which there are two types: perforate and imperforate. Perforate coral has a porous skeleton through which the polyps connect to each other while imperforate corals have solid, isolated skeletons. Using this basic structure each species forms its own distinctive shape. The skeletons are composed of miniscule deposits of aragonite, a form of calcium carbonate, which the polyps collect from calcium ions in sea water.

Individual polyps are only a few millimeters in diameter and are made up of two cell layers; the epidermis, or outer skin, and the gastrodermis – the internal, tubular, jelly-like body which has a central mouth surrounded by radial symmetrical tentacles. The polyp is encased in a corallite exoskeleton (scientifically called the theca) into which it can retreat at will.

▶ *A coral reef is comprised of many different types of colored and shaped coral.*

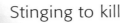

Stinging to kill

The number of tentacles differs according to the species but they all carry stinging cells with which to catch and immobilize prey. Food is then passed into the mouth and directly to the gut with any waste matter expelled back through the same route in little puffs of matter. During daylight hours most corals keep their tentacles withdrawn to avoid being eaten by predators such as fire worms, snails, sea urchins, parrot fish and butterfly fish. At night the distinctive waving polyps re-appear to catch microscopic zooplankton rising up to the ocean surface.

As well as zooplankton and tiny fish, corals absorb nutrients from seawater and inorganic nitrogen and phosphorus. As discussed above, they benefit from the presence of sponges growing in reef crevices – so-called 'filter feeders' – because these absorb phytoplankton and then excrete nutrients for corals to feed on. Sponges also provide shelter for fish, crabs, shrimp and many other small animals.

However the corals' most important source of food and oxygen – up to 90 per cent – comes from the symbiotic single-celled algae called zooxanthellae. These live within the polyp's gut tissues in a union called endosymbiosis.

Zooxanthellae absorb solar energy using photosynthesis and supply the polyp with organic nutrients in the form of glycerol, glucose and amino acids. In return the zooxanthellae collect the carbon dioxide and nitrogenous waste produced by the polyp and use them for photosynthesis. Coral reefs grow much quicker in zones of strong sunlight because this symbiotic relationship relies on good photosynthesis.

It also provides coral with its color but if food becomes scarce or there are other environmental pressures the polyp may eject the zooxanthellae from its exoskeleton. This results in a draining of color, a condition known as coral bleaching. Unless the symbiotic algae return, both polyp and coral will die.

Polyps can be male, female or hermaphrodite and may change sex as they mature. Asexual reproduction can occur after a storm when large pieces of coral are broken off and borne by currents to suitable anchorages. Branching corals often multiply in this way; the new colonies are clones of the original.

◀ *Orange sun coral with its tentacles extended for feeding.*

▶ *This mushroom soft coral is pale in color due to lack of any symbiotic algae (Zooxanthellae).*

▶ *Brain corals extend their tentacles to catch food at night but use them for protection by wrapping them over the grooves on their surface during the day.*

Growth occurs in a number of ways but many species use 'budding'. This process can either be intratenticular, in which a bud grows from the oral discs of the old polyp, as in brain corals (*Diploria* spp.), or extratenticular budding, where it forms at the base of the old polyp; this is the preferred method for bolder corals (*Montastraea* spp.).

Many other marine animals contribute to the growth of coral reefs. Creatures such as tube worms and mollusks leave their hard, calcium-rich skeletons behind when they die and these become incorporated into the reef by coralline algae. This alga slowly deposits thin sheets of limestone over the surface of the coral and, in so doing, cements together all calcium detritus left by other creatures. Its work greatly contributes to the structural integrity and strength of the reef, especially at the leading edge facing the open ocean.

▲ *Here, Christmas tree worms are seen as feather-like structures, embedded in yellow coral.*

Spawn Clouds

However, most reef corals reproduce sexually by the synchronous spawning of male sperm and female eggs. Here one or more species simultaneously release great clouds of spawn, usually after a full moon and ideally in spring. Temperature conditions have to be perfect for mass spawning, with little level change between high and low tides, and once begun it can last anywhere between a few minutes and 48 hours. The eggs float to the surface where they are fertilized and become dispersed over a large area. The fertilized egg (zygote) then develops into a larva, attaching itself to the sea bed or other suitable surface from where it will produce a new colony.

Reefs tend to grow in spurts with occasional 'resting' periods which seem to be associated with recovery after storm damage. On a much smaller but nevertheless important scale, grazing and boring organisms such as Christmas tree worms (*Spirobranchus giganteus*) break corals down into fine sand which infiltrates and fills gaps between reefs. These 'bioeroders' include species such as sea urchins, sponges and 'grazers' like parrotfish.

▼ *Stony corals spawn each March at the Ningaloo Reef in Western Australia.*

Defining life on the reef

Established reefs have different zones of light and wave action governing the types of organism which live there. There are three distinct zones – the reef crest, the fore-reef and the reef flat.

The reef crest lies at or near the ocean surface and receives both the most light and the worst battering from wind and waves. It is home to robust, sharp corals able to cope with the erosive action of incessantly breaking waves.

The fore-reef faces the open ocean and is composed of three levels; a top level of sharp, branching coral which grows just below the surface, a middle section of larger, more rounded corals and, at the base, a flattish coral which spreads along the deep and dark leading edge. To capture as much sunlight as possible it forms great, horizontal, plate-like masses.

The reef flat, which can be a lagoon behind the main structure, lies in generally shallow, calm waters and comprises coral fragments, limestone and sand. This area is mercilessly exposed to intense sunshine, which means hotter water temperatures and therefore a higher saline content – conditions which severely limit the species able to survive.

▼ *Table corals are most common in shallow reef environments with bright light and moderate to high water motion.*

Coral reef fish tend to be highly colorful and often occupy a specialized role within the ecosystem. Some, like the parrotfish (*Scaridae* spp.) and butterflyfish (*Chaetodontidae* spp.) feed on the coral itself while others such as wrasses (*Labridae* spp.) live off seaweed or small animals.

◄ Collared butterflyfish in this coral reef in the Maldives.

Some fish act as ocean orthodontists, cleaning the remnants of food from the jaws of their larger, predatory cousins. Then there are the specialist sea-urchin and seaweed consumers such as damselfish (*Pomacentridae* spp.) while fish living along the margins of the coral reef, or in nearby seagrass meadows, tend to be more predatory in nature. These include various types of shark, barracuda (*Sphyraena* spp.) and snapper as well as groupers (*Epinephelus* spp.) pompanos (*Trachinotus* spp.) and manta rays.

This wonderfully varied population helps keep coral reefs within delicate ecological boundaries; too many of one species and the knock-on effect causes problems for the entire ecosystem. If, for instance, the sea urchin Diadema antillarum begins to lose numbers the algae on which it feeds could run riot, suffocating coral across the reef.

▼ The fore-reef of a perpendicular wall dive site at Christmas Island, Australia.

Poisoners on the loose

Given the above, it goes without saying that the reef is a dangerous place for many marine animals – especially when a predator as formidable as the sea snake is hungry. These venomous creatures are found in warm coastal waters from the Indian Ocean to the Pacific and coral reefs are a favorite hunting ground. They tend to roam around the reef rather than within it and their small heads and thin necks allow them to move easily between the coral.

The Great Barrier Reef is a particularly attractive haunt for them and supports at least 17 species. These include the light blue banded sea snake (*Laticauda colubrine*), which eats fish and fish eggs, cuttlefish, crabs, eels and squid, and the venomous olive sea snake (*Aipysurus laevis*) which grows to a nightmarish 1.8 m (6 ft) long. However, in the oceans it is a big mistake to necessarily equate size with danger. The blue ringed octopus (*Hapalochlaena lunulata*) is only 20 cm (8 in) long but is arguably the deadliest of all octopuses. It is found in the shallow reefs of Indonesia, Australia, New Guinea and the Philippines where it preys on wounded fish and invertebrates, lying in wait among the crevices and rocks until its victim appears. It then emerges with astonishing speed, snagging victims with its tentacles before using its tough beak to bite and deliver a deadly neurotoxin (nerve poison) via its saliva. The poison, maculotoxin, is strong enough to kill an adult human.

Sea turtles such as the green (*Chelonia mydas*), hawksbill (*Eretmochelys imbricata*) and loggerhead (*Caretta caretta*) are coral reef visitors which relish browsing on a rich and varied diet. They are carnivorous and particularly enjoy eating jellyfish (although they will also take sponges, corals, crustaceans and small fish).

Sea anemones are part of the Actiniaria family and fellow members of the phylum Cnidaria. They are close relatives of both corals and jellyfish and share characteristics such as stinging tentacles and soft bodies. Scientifically classified as stinging polyps, they attach themselves to coral reefs or rocks on the sea bed and lie in wait for passing fish.

Sea anemones have symmetrical bodies featuring an adhesive base disc, a cylindrical, columnar-shaped body and numerous tentacles around a central slit-shaped mouth (which doubles up as an anus). Tentacles vary in number from about 30 to many hundreds and are highly sensitive to movement. They snatch prey – usually small fish and shrimp – and immediately fire a harpoon-like filament into their victim to inject a paralyzing neurotoxin. The tentacles then pull the stunned prey into the mouth. Crustaceans prey on sea anemones but are susceptible to their poison.

▼ *With almost perfect camouflage, this greater blue-ringed octopus is one of the world's most venomous animals.*

On coral reefs Clownfish (*Amphiprioninae* spp.) share a symbiotic relationship with these curious creatures. They live in small groups inside the anemone, usually a male and female pair plus a couple of immature fish, where they are protected from predators by the stinging tentacles (to which they are immune). The fish eat the small invertebrates, and probably parasites, which would otherwise attack the anemone, and expel fecal matter to provide their host with important nutrients.

Sea anemones sometimes move short distances but rarely do so unless threatened, in which case they can swim away by flexing their body. They reproduce asexually in three ways; by budding, by division of the polyp into two sections (binary fission), or where a piece of the pedal disc breaks off and regenerates into small anemones. They can also reproduce sexually by producing sperm and eggs ejected through their mouths. A fertilized egg becomes a larva which swims to a new home where it anchors and grows into a single polyp.

▲ *A hawksbill sea turtle eats organ pipe coral; note the tissue burns around its face from the stinging coral.*

▼ *These blackfinned clownfish are safe among the stinging tentacles their Magnificent Anemone host.*

◄ A crown of thorns starfish feeds on corals in the Sea of Cortez.

Killer starfish – the crown of thorns

One of the biggest natural predators of coral polyps is the crown of thorns starfish (*Acanthaster planci*). These creatures inhabit coral reefs in the Indian and Pacific oceans, along with the Red Sea, and when present in large enough numbers can devastate reefs, leaving only dead coral skeletons in their wake.

The crown of thorns is a solitary animal, usually feeding at night when the polyps emerge. However during population explosions, when competition for food is rife, it will feed in daylight hours as well. The starfish can grow up to 50 cm (1.6 ft) in diameter and have anything from 13 to 16 arms covered with sharp spines about 5 cm (1.9 in) long which it uses to defend itself. These 'thorns', from which it takes its name, are viciously sharp and venomous and contain a powerful neurotoxin.

This carnivorous predator feeds by climbing onto a reef and then everting its stomach through its mouth. The 'inside out' stomach sac completely covers the chosen piece of coral, which it then digests by liquefying the polyp with enzymes. This allows the starfish to absorb nutrients.

The crown of thorns is a voracious feeder, consuming as much as 6 square meters (65 square feet) of coral reef annually. Despite this enormous appetite it can survive for six months without eating; one of several attributes which make it such a difficult species to control. It spawns millions of eggs every year and, once fertilized, these become larvae within a day and can swim to colonize new areas of reef. Within a month the larva grows into a five-armed juvenile and after two years is mature enough to reproduce. The starfish can even regenerate a new animal from a severed limb.

Before it became a marine pest it is thought that the crown of thorns was important for controlling the growth of fast growing coral, so allowing slower species time to establish. However it became notorious for widespread damage wreaked on the Great Barrier Reef and more recently across Tubbataha Reef near the Philippines. Relatively recent population explosions (since about 1970) are tentatively blamed on environmental pollution, specifically fresh water containing agricultural 'run-off' (fertilizers) which promotes algal blooms and subsequent excessive growth in certain species.

The crown of thorns does have a few natural enemies – some large fish eat them, together with the giant triton (*Charonia tritonis*) and harlequin shrimp (*Gnathophyllidae* spp.). But scientists believe over-fishing of these predators has become another factor in the apparently relentless growth in numbers. There is no obvious control for this species (although marine biologists are trying hard to find one) and a population 'outbreak' can easily last for between one and five years – even 20 years if food is abundant. It takes at least a decade for a reef to recover from a crown of thorns attack, if it recovers at all.

Reefs on the edge of survival

Coral reefs are vulnerable because they thrive only in a narrow range of environmental conditions and, although apparently solid, are fragile and easily broken. Rough seas and winds, especially hurricanes, can wreak massive damage on brittle coral within hours and over-enthusiastic divers and snorkelers – lured by a tourism industry seeking to sell the beauty of reefs – are a perpetual long-term threat. In the past unscrupulous or uneducated tourists have broken off pieces of coral through carelessness or to sell as souvenirs. More recently an active and illegal trade in coral reef species has emerged, with colorful fish as prized as the coral itself.

Individual corals, sometimes entire reef systems, suffer from diseases linked to environmental stress. Earlier we looked at a condition known as coral bleaching where the symbiotic zooxanthellae algae die and the coral loses its color. The exact causes of mass bleachings are not fully understood but are thought to occur through disease, pollution such as raw sewage, loss of light, increased radiation, sedimentation and reduced salinity caused by heavy rain. But the commonest cause is increased water temperature or a rapidly fluctuating temperature, both associated with climate change. Furthermore, increasing acidification of the oceans, caused by rising carbon dioxide levels, is making it harder for corals to build their calcium-based skeletons.

Coral colonies can withstand bleaching for about two weeks – and sometimes recover if the cause of the stress disappears – but will otherwise die. When this happens all animals in the ecosystem suffer (even the larger fish disappear) and the area becomes almost barren of marine life. Dead coral turns white but can in time form the substrata for new colonies if conditions recover.

While it's true that human activity is often to blame for destroying these vibrant ecosystems, it would be wrong to attribute the problem wholly to the industrialized world. Sometimes people in poor coastal communities are just trying to make a living, or unknowingly destroy reefs by removing larger corals for building. But, whatever the reasons, the facts are frightening. Scientists estimate that two-thirds of the world's coral reefs are at risk and that they are already disappearing at the rate of 2 per cent each year.

Since the catastrophic Indian Ocean tsunami of December 26, 2004, oceanographers have discovered that coral reefs are far more than just amazing structures and ecosystems. It

▶ *Coral reefs are fragile environments; here dead coral has been destroyed by waves.*

appears they provide a vital defense against destructive tidal waves, absorbing much of the energy and deflecting a wave's direction away from the land. This was clearly demonstrated in a 2006 study which showed that where reefs had been destroyed the land beyond suffered disproportionately more than in areas where reefs still existed. Tsumanis apart, coral reefs provide a daily defense against sea erosion for the coastlines and islands they surround.

▶ *This large colony of staghorn coral suffers from an extensive bleached area at its center.*

◄ Twobar anemone fish on a coral-covered shipwreck in the Red Sea.

▶ Palmyra Atoll, the scene of an environmental catastrophe.

A ships' graveyard

The sharp surfaces and spear-like projections common to coral reefs have proved lethal to shipping over the years. Because the upper levels lie just below the surface, reefs are hidden from immediate view unless surf is actually breaking on them. Even then, strong currents can push unprepared mariners onto the unforgiving rocks.

Leaving aside the risk to human life, reef shipwrecks are now thought to have long-term consequences for the coral. Rusting hulks provide a haven for marine plants and animals but can also introduce unwanted species into the ecosystem. This upsets the delicate relationship balance within the reef; foreign organisms such as algae, for instance, become rampant in such a rich environment if there are no predators around.

The most notorious contemporary example of 'wreck vandalism' lies in the remote central Pacific atoll of Palmyra, where the hulk of a 30 m (100 ft) vessel which ran aground in 1991 has led directly led to the rapid growth of the alien species *Rhodactis howesii*. This organism, with its stinging tentacles, is related to corals and sea anemones but is now overwhelming the atoll, smothering established coral and killing it. Remarkably, it seems to double its territory annually and where there were once diverse species there is now a monoculture of the invader. Scientists from the US Geological Survey think that iron leaching from the shipwreck is helping it grow and that the organism has taken too strong a hold to make removal of the wreck worthwhile.

However, shipwrecks are not always bad news. In the Red Sea they have become transformed into artificial reefs – thriving habitats for a diverse range of creatures and coral colonies. Initially fish will colonize a wreck but in the right conditions coral will slowly start to build up, especially where there is a steel hull. Steel is quickly covered by calcareous algae which in turn gives coral larvae a suitable grounding for growth.

Artificial reefs provide a home for some of the rarer corals which lack the ability to compete against vigorous, established species in natural settings. They also present a viable and exciting alternative site for divers, so reducing 'human stress' on natural reefs.

INDEX

NB: page numbers in italic indicate illustrations

PICTURE CREDITS

The publisher would like to thank FLPA - images of nature and their photographers for supplying all the pictures for the interior of this book. They would like to thank FLPA, Corbis and ThinkStock for cover images.

Front Cover: Gray Hardel/Corbis, iStockphoto/ThinkStock (x2), Tom Brakefield/Stockbyte/ThinkStock
Back Cover/Jacket: Chris Newbert/Minden Pictures/FLPA (Back Cover); Chris Newbert/Minden Pictures/FLPA (Inside front cover flap); iStockPhoto/ThinkStock (Inside back cover flap); Comstock/ThinkStock (Back Cover)

Front end paper: Jurgen & Christine Sohns/FLPA
Back end paper: Reinhard Dirscherl/FLPA

J W Alker/Imagebroker/FLPA: 130-131, 138, 199, 210; Ingo Arndt/ Minden Pictures/FLPA: 82, 83; Fred Bavendam/Minden Pictures/FLPA: 30, 76-77, 80-81, 98, 99 top, 103, 111 top, 120 bottom, 134-135, 148, 183, 209 top, 212-213, 219 bottom; Ed Bowlby, NOAA/Olympic Coast NMS; NOAA/OAR/Office of Ocean Exploration: 141; Luciano Candisani/ Minden Pictures/FLPA: 159; Jonathan Carlile/Imagebroker/FLPA: 62; Christiana Carvalho/FLPA: 66-67; Tui De Roy/Minden Pictures/FLPA: 36, 74 bottom, 121 top, 191, 194, 221; Jacques Descloitres, MODIS Land Science Team/NASA : 20-21; Michael Dietrich/Imagebroker/FLPA: 22; Reinhard Dirscherl/FLPA: Back end papers, 1, 2, 4, 6-7, 11, 42, 74 top, 88-89, 97 bottom, 108, 109 top, 126 both, 127 bottom, 150 top, 171 top, 172-173, 174 top, 175 bottom, 182-183, 184, 188-189, 190, 192 top, 193, 196, 200-201, 204, 205-206, 213, 214, 214-215, 220-221; Suzi Eszterhas/ Minden Pictures/FLPA: 76, 146; FB-Fischer/Imagebroker/FLPA: 54; Foto Natura Stock/FLPA: 106-107, 150 bottom, 152 bottom; Mark Franklin: 10 left, 13, 15, 23 top, 26, 28, 40 both, 43, 46 right, 49, 55, 59, 65, 93, 94 top; Bob Gibbons/FLPA: 164; Michael Gore/FLPA: 206; David T. Grewcock/ FLPA: 99 bottom; Richard Herrmann/Minden Pictures/FLPA: 82-83; Paul Hobson/FLPA: 140; Michio Hoshino/Minden Pictures/FLPA: 158-159; David Hosking/FLPA: 68 top, 75 top; ImageBroker/Imagebroker/FLPA: 24, 37, 96, 124-125, 127 top, 138-139, 166-167, 175 top, 198-199, 208 bottom, 209 bottom, 212 top, 219 top; Mitsuaki Iwago/Minden Pictures/ FLPA: 208 top; S Jonasson/FLPA: 35 top; Gerard Lacz/FLPA: 110 bottom, 120 top; Wolfgang Lampe/Imagebroker/FLPA: 62-63; Frank W Lane/ FLPA: 88, 100 bottom; Frans Lanting/FLPA: 44-45, 155, 165 top; Hans Leijnse/FN/Minden/FLPA: 115; Scott Leslie/Minden Pictures/FLPA: 33, 78-79, 132; Linda Lewis/FLPA: 100 top; Oliver Lucanus/Minden Pictures/ FLPA: 202-203; Colin Marshall/FLPA: 75 bottom, 92, 101, 168, 171 bottom, 192 bottom, 197, 215; Steve McCutcheon/FLPA: 56; Wil Meinderts/FN/ Minden/FLPA: 114 bottom; Hiroya Minakuchi/Minden Pictures/FLPA: 70-71, 102, 110 top, 113 top, 144, 147 top; Yva Momatiuk & John Eastcott/

Minden Pictures/FLPA: 12-13, 50-51, 64-65, 68-69, 154 bottom, 161 top; Colin Monteath/Minden Pictures/FLPA: 60-61; Colin Munro/FLPA: 16 top, 123; NASA: 8-9, 41, 57; NASA Goddard's Scientific Visualization Studio: 58-59; Piotr Naskrecki/Minden Pictures/FLPA: 84; Chris Newbert/

Minden Pictures/FLPA: 38-39, 86-87, 94 bottom, 139, 176, 206-207, 216; Mark Newman/FLPA: 46 left, 107, 112 bottom, 160; Flip Nicklin/Minden Pictures/FLPA: 25 bottom, 26-27, 90, 122, 125, 142-143, 154 top, 165 bottom, 186, 195 bottom; NOAA: 25 top, 35 bottom; Michael Quinton/ Minden Pictures/FLPA: 113 bottom; Pete Oxford/Minden Pictures/FLPA: 97 top, 157; Panda Photo/FLPA: 121 bottom, 133; Mike Parry/Minden Pictures/FLPA: 114 top, 151 top, 195 top; Fritz Polking/FLPA: 153; Norbert Probst/Imagebroker/FLPA: 118-119, 137, 149; QuikScat/NASA: 23 bottom; Cyril Ruoso/Minden Pictures/FLPA: 156, 162; Kevin Schafer/Minden Pictures/FLPA: 152; Malcolm Schuyl/FLPA: 47; Silvestris Fotoservice/FLPA: 14-15; Don Smith/FLPA: 72; Gary K Smith/FLPA: 31; Jurgen & Christine Sohns/FLPA: Front end papers, 145; Sunset/FLPA: 147 bottom
Steve Trewhella/FLPA: 32, 73; US Geological Survey: 10 right; Jan Van Arkel/FN/Minden/FLPA: 177, 179; Rinie Van Meurs/FN/Minden/FLPA: 161 bottom; Peter Verhoog/FN/Minden/FLPA: 116, 117; Jan Vermeer/Minden Pictures/FLPA: 158; Birgitte Wilms/Minden Pictures/FLPA: 174 bottom; D P Wilson/FLPA: 19, 79, 173, 178, 181, 187; Winfried Wisniewski/FLPA: 48, 104-105; Norbert Wu/Minden Pictures/FLPA: 16 bottom, 17 both, 18, 28-29, 52, 53, 85, 91 both, 95, 109 bottom, 111 bottom, 112 top, 128 both, 136-137, 163, 169, 170, 172, 180-181, 185, 201, 211, 217 both, 218.

Every effort has been made to trace the ownership of copyrighted material and to secure permission from copyright holders. In the event of any question arising as to the use of any material, we will be pleased to make any necessary corrections in future printings.

Project Managed by BlueRed Press Ltd